"Francine Watkins has penned a very good lesson book about how to live life. She simply disguises it as a terrific book on sales leadership. Her journey starts with a determined young woman hell bent on becoming a top leader in party plan sales. As she gains success, she discovers that sales skills are only part of what is required. To really succeed one must learn how to get others to follow . . . one must lead. In a frank and easy to comprehend fashion Francine shares how she transformed ambition and determination into a skill set that elevated her to one of the truly gifted leader/teacher/communicators in direct selling history."

—W. ALAN LUCE, *CEO, Wildtree, Inc., past chairman of the Direct Selling Association and inductee into the DSA Hall of Fame*

"What a wonderful tool for any and every person in direct sales! . . . The book is relevant, contemporary, and comprehensive. You have not missed a thing."

—PAULA ANTONINI, *global director, The Body Shop at Home; member of DSA Board of Directors*

"I've read many a how-to book, but often found myself looking for something new. *From the Ground Up* is just that book. It will prove invaluable to anyone in sales."

—SYLVIA BOYD, *past president, Tupperware Canada*

"In the world of coaches and trainers, *From the Ground Up* is like having a personal trainer available to me twenty-four-seven."

—JEAN ANN DOLAN, *regional director of Field Development, Kara Vita*

"*From the Ground Up* is a reference book to be used again and again by anyone in sales."

—JERRY O' CONNOR, *president, O'Connor and Associates*

"Especially wonderful are the author's personal stories from her many years on the front lines of direct sales."

—STEPHANIE CULP, *author, lecturer, seminar leader, and founding member and past president of the National Association of Professional Organizers*

**the lift you need to
succeed in DIRECT SALES**

from the **UP**
groundUP

Francine Watkins

Published by Selling Edge Publishing
PO Box 785, Oceanville, New Jersey 08231

Design and composition by Greenleaf Book Group LP
Cover design by Greenleaf Book Group LP

Library of Congress Control Number: 2006926204

Publisher's Catloging-in-Publication Data:
Watkins, Francine.
   From the ground up : the lift you need to succeed in direct sales / Francine Watkins.—st ed.
   p. ; cm.
   ISBN-13: 978-0-9779995-0-7
   ISBN-10: 0-9779995-0-5
   1. Direct selling. 2. Sales management. 3. Sales personnel—Handbooks, manuals, etc. I. Title.
   HF5438.25 .W38 2006
   658.8/72 2006926204

Printed in the United States of America on acid-free paper

08 09 10 11 12   10 9 8 7 6 5 4 3 2

First Edition

To Alfred, my rock. My forever gratitude for giving me love, security, respect, and protection—always.

To Stephen and Lori, my sunshine.
Joyful when you walk through the door,
sad when you leave.

CONTENTS

ACKNOWLEDGMENTS

My gratitude to the amazing people who touched my life and helped me grow:

Paula Antonini is smart, quick to learn, focused, resilient, and above all, loyal. She remembers those who helped her along the way. She richly deserves her phenomenal success.

Sylvia Boyd is the ultimate professional saleswoman. She has contributed *much* to the growth of her company, with class and style. Sylvia shared some priceless wisdom from her vast years of experience.

Dr. Peter Chamberlain, for believing in me and this book *way* before the fact and for helping me visualize the end result.

Rosemary Cinque, a woman of deep faith and phenomenal courage. Rosemary taught me to appreciate and respect the beauty all around me. Rosemary is an inspiration to everyone fortunate enough to know her. Many top sales performers have Rosemary to thank for helping them succeed.

Stephanie Culp, my talented curmudgeon buddy, who knew exactly what to cut, what to keep, and what to move. (She hides her generous heart well.)

Jean Ann Dolan, naturally talented, creative, funny, loving, and a dynamic positive force for all those whose lives she touches.

Joe Hara, for giving me the opportunity of a lifetime, an opportunity that had an enormous, positive impact on me and on my family.

Landis Haugen whose love, respect, and strong belief in the value of my training (and willingness to shout it from the rooftops) will never be forgotten.

Barbara Jack, warm, caring, and giving, and an outstanding example of a "purpose-driven" leader.

Cheryl Lafevre, my bright, gentle, generous college buddy who fought the good fight and is now helping some slow learner in heaven.

Ann Layman, my forever friend, is a gutsy, take-charge survivor with a tender, giving heart.

Jack Linn, for identifying and touting my talents early in the game.

Alan Luce, for giving me the opportunity to expand my knowledge of direct sales in a whole new environment and especially for trusting that I would be up to the task.

Michelle Masterson, the quintessential professional. She has the courage to speak her mind. There seems to be no end to her abilities. I'm in awe of her. How *rich* I have been to have her in my life for so many years.

Pat Molnar, who taught me to think, to question, to stretch. Pat's high standards, inquisitive mind, glorious sense of humor, love of family, friends, and nature set her apart. A dear and loving friend, gone *much* too soon, missed forever.

Jerry O'Connor, thank you for pulling me into the twenty-first century and giving so generously of your time and vast knowledge. A caring gentleman and a loyal friend.

Julia Sicilano, my dear aunt who can always separate the wheat from the chaff. She's the poster child for unconditional love.

Diana Swenson is a bright, funny, resilient, and scrupulously honest leader. Diana has been a loyal buddy for over forty years. She's still pushing me to grow.

Sharon Weaver, my detail guru and caring friend. Sharon is blessed with a glorious organized mind and high standards. What would I have done without her logical thinking?

To Cecile Wray, my leveler, my constant, my dear friend, in good times and bad; and to Howie, for pushing me to find that "fire in my belly."

I've learned from many of the best. My appreciation goes to just some of the professionals I've known personally through my work or whose seminars and presentations I've attended: Maria Arapakis, Mary Kay Ash, Leo Buscaglia, Dr. Stephen R. Covey, Stephanie Culp, Rita Davenport, Dr. Wayne Dyer, Alan Lakein, Ken Miller, Dr. Sheila Murray Bethel, Rosita Perez, Anthony Robbins, Marsha Sinetar, Denis Waitley, Jack Welch, and Zig Ziglar.

To the dealers and managers of Sky Hi Sales for the privilege of knowing and working with you.

To the thousands of direct salespeople who have taught me that decency and hard work *can* pay off.

To my amazing team in the corporate world—those men and women who willingly shared their abundant creativity, their knowledge, and their talent.

Thank you to five exceptional mentors for their guidance and support: Chuck Elwell, Alan Luce, Ken Miller, Pat Molnar, and Gordon Shave.

To the classy, talented folks at Greenleaf Book Group who were dedicated to making this book fly.

Gratitude to Nana, Bill, and Bud Holden for their early nurturing and "protection from the storm."

To Mom, for passing on the "will to survive" gene.

To my incredibly talented children, Lori and Stephen, for their love and encouragement—and just for *being*.

Thank you Donald Pettifer, my cheerleader, my sage, my love. This book never would have been without you.

The Proud Profession of Selling

Be Proud of What You Do

You're holding this book because you're either thinking about selling or you're already involved in direct sales. Good for you! In this exciting profession, it's possible to make an enormous amount of money, keep your autonomy, and meet phenomenal people. And best of all, you can have all that without sacrificing your integrity. That's one impressive package. But it took time and experience to lead me to this conclusion. It certainly was not how I felt initially.

When I first started in direct sales, no way did I see myself as a salesperson. I was embarrassed to tell family and friends. I skirted around the word *selling*. I said things like, "This is kind of a hobby." Yeah, right, a hobby—so I could help my hardworking husband meet our overwhelming expenses. "I'm demonstrating a product I really believe in. I just want a chance to introduce it to your friends.

No one's obligated to buy." Baloney! I was counting on their buying, but as long as I didn't *say* it, I didn't have to acknowledge to myself that I was SELLING! I worried that others would question the sincerity of my naturally friendly, outgoing personality once they discovered I wanted to "sell them something." Perhaps I felt that way because I associated sales with the timeworn image of the sleazy used-car salesman. (My apologies to the honest men and women who sell used cars.) Maybe it was because I'd heard about the slick guys who breeze into town, convince the little old lady she needs her driveway coated, then sneak out of town before the next rain washes the coating away. I'm sure my attitude was influenced by my few bad experiences with salespeople. (It takes only a couple of negatives to draw a lifelong conclusion.) Whatever the reasons, I was dead wrong.

The vast majority of salespeople I know—and I know hundreds personally—are hardworking, honest, caring professionals who believe strongly in the value of what they're selling. Are there unscrupulous salespeople out there? Sure. Will they be successful some of the time? Yes. But there are many more of the good guys. Hats off to you for being one of them. And when you're feeling insecure, remember this: The world *needs* us, because no matter how outstanding the product or service, no matter how sophisticated the distribution system, *nothing happens until somebody sells something.*

So whether you're new to sales or tops in your field, remind yourself that our whole economy is based on the skills and efforts of salespeople—*your* skills and efforts.

I sure wish someone had given me the following advice years ago:

> *Be proud of what you do.*

Using This Book

I can only imagine the number of things you could be doing right now, but you've chosen to read this book. So please, use it and abuse it. Think of it as a kind of personal seminar, one you attend whenever you choose.

This book starts at the beginning—inside the salesperson's head—and leads the way through getting started, closing a sale, managing a successful business, leading a team, and even developing leaders. If you're new to direct sales, the first ten chapters are all about you, the salesperson. But don't stop reading when I start explaining how to lead other salespeople. That could be you sooner than you think! If you're a seasoned veteran, you may be tempted to skip to the parts about leading and growing your business. Please don't do that. Reviewing the basics might just remind you of the one small idea you haven't used that can make a *big* difference in your results.

> *I've found that often it isn't what I don't know that hurts me— it's what I know and don't practice that does me in.*

Besides that, the first parts of the book make a great resource for teaching those you take under your wing.

Now that I've convinced you to stick with me all the way, let's review some helpful suggestions for getting the most out of your time. Take it at your own speed. If reading one chapter at a time, or even one section at a time, works for you, that's fine. If you get an insight and want to make a change before moving on, that's fine too. If you and a buddy want to focus on each chapter together, discuss it, and act on ideas little by little, that's *also* perfectly fine. In fact, there's considerable benefit to discussing your thoughts and reactions with someone else: it's stimulating, it clarifies your thinking, and it opens the door to additional ideas.

Whenever you're reading, have a highlighter, pencil, and sticky notes handy. When you read an idea that clicks, highlight it. When you have a related thought you want to remember, jot it down in the margin. Use sticky notes to mark the pages you know will help you. It will sure beat thumbing through a whole section to find one small thing later on.

You'll find exercises throughout the book. Please don't blow them off. They're there to make you think about, act on, and benefit from the information in each chapter. Go to my Web site, **www.directsellingedge.com**, and print the forms you'll need to write down your comments. Put them in a binder. Then follow the instructions in each chapter. If you don't have easy access to a computer, don't let that stop you. Simply make chapter headings on blank paper, put *those* in your binder, and you're ready to go.

Why am I so adamant about you taking this step? Unless you act on what you've learned, you will likely not act at all! I know from experience. I've attended many a training session, taken copious notes, and never opened the book again. (Sound familiar?) Every time I've conducted a seminar, I've reminded myself of this painfully humbling fact: Even though the audience's enthusiastic applause is heartwarming, even though many single me out afterward to tell me how much they learned, I *know* that unless they take some action within a brief time, nothing will change. It's human nature to forget all those good intentions once we're in the midst of real world demands.

As you read on, you'll notice that I've used *she* most often because throughout my career I've worked mostly with women. But the information in this book is just as relevant for men who choose sales, either as a full-time career or as a second income. And husband-and-wife teams have proven to be a powerful force in many direct sales organizations.

I've also used conversational language throughout. I want you to feel as though I'm talking directly to you—because I am. And if,

from time to time, you find yourself answering out loud or chuck-
ling, that's great. We've *connected*!

Success Is Up to You

Remember that wherever and however you started in *no way*
determines what you can accomplish. I've seen excited, personable new people who have had an outstanding beginning in sales,
mostly because several of their friends and family were willing to
give them a start. Many didn't last when they had to draw on their
own strengths.

Others struggled from the start. One in particular comes to
mind. Cecelia had recently given up a singing career that had
kept her on the road, so she didn't have a large local network
of friends to help her. At her first presentation she sold seven-
teen dollars' worth of merchandise. Considering her overhead,
the presentation cost her considerably more than she made, and
her hopes for future business were mighty dim. But she simply
refused to give up. Thanks to her hard work and sheer desire to
succeed, Cecelia went on to become a manager and was awarded
a company car.

In my case, I had two young children and *zero* sales experience.
But after I hosted a demonstration, I figured out the demonstrator must have cleared at least fifteen dollars. Since I loved the
products, I decided to give selling a try. Those were lean times,
and a few presentations a month would go a *long* way toward
helping my husband pay the mortgage on our first home. I didn't
know what I was doing, I had no idea how long I would last, and
if someone had told me that I would end up training top sales
leaders internationally and eventually head the training department of the Fortune 500 company I represented, I would have
laughed out loud! Much of what I've learned on that exhilarating, rewarding, and sometimes painful journey is in this book.

Do I have all the answers? Certainly not. Do I have many that may be worthy of your time? *You bet.*

> One idea, one insight, one reminder can mean
> the difference between hanging in or hanging it up;
> between making it, or making it big.

CHAPTER 1

Get Ready: You Have What It Takes

Before we get to the nitty-gritty, I want to assure you that no matter how new you are to sales, no matter how much you have yet to learn, no matter how little success you have had, none of it determines what you can accomplish in the future. You can learn, do, and be whatever you aim for in sales. One of my favorite lyrics from a Broadway musical says it beautifully: "It's not where you start, it's where you finish."

The beginning of my sales career wasn't exactly sterling. Business didn't fall in my lap. I started by asking family and friends to host a presentation. Several people I was *sure* would help me didn't. (Still smarts.) Surprisingly, some I hardly knew said yes. I went door-to-door "friend finding" to ask for business. I was so frightened that when I knocked, I hoped and prayed no one would answer.

For my first presentations, I was dressed professionally, I was enthusiastic about the product, and I followed the company's suggestions to the letter. No flies on me. One pip of a problem: Of the more than a dozen presentations I held, I couldn't schedule even *one* new one. After so many noes I began to feel beaten up—and beaten down.

Then a miracle happened. With just a few hours' notice, my manager called and said she was unable to hold a presentation near me. She asked if I'd be willing to hold it. I could hardly keep from saying, "You've gotta be kidding. You bet I'm willing!" It turned out to be my saving grace. Everything finally clicked. They laughed, they liked me, they bought, and most importantly, I scheduled two future events. Hallelujah! Although my future was hanging by a thread, I was still in business.

But something much more significant had happened. That one positive experience got me thinking, *I can do this.* I needed the money, wanted badly to succeed, and I began to believe I could!

Why was that presentation different? Why did I click with those guests? For one thing, unlike my initial presentations, the guests weren't people I knew, so I wasn't out-psyched by my audience. Second, they were a fun-loving group and my personality meshed with theirs, and perhaps the most important reason of all was that I just relaxed, had fun, and let it happen. My focus, for the *first time,* was on the guests and not on me. That was my turning point.

What's the secret? Why do some go on to phenomenal success while others give up after little effort? What distinguishes them from the rest of the world? Can you pick them out in a crowd?

What a Salesperson Looks Like

Were I to list just *some* characteristics of several top sales performers, it would read something like this:

short / tall
thin / wholesome
college educated / high school dropout

lives in a city / a small town / the country
outgoing / shy
experienced worker / little or no work experience
male / female
financially independent / modest income

My point is that those who succeed can't be neatly categorized by the obvious. Not one of the above characteristics is a reason for success, or an excuse for failure.

I remember one gentle, soft-spoken national top-ten sales leader who was so shy that she seemed to be in physical pain when she was asked to share some of her ideas. She spoke in a whisper. She looked fragile. We marveled at how she had ever had the fortitude and courage to build such an impressive sales organization. Perhaps it was because of her strong belief in the product, or her quiet sincerity, or because others were drawn to her. Perhaps it was all three.

I've been thrown off many times by making snap judgments. I vividly recall my first reaction when I interviewed Sally, a charming gray-haired lady. Her home was magnificent. Her husband was a successful executive. She was active in her community. She had it all—or so I thought.

I was *convinced* that the only reason Sally was even considering joining the company was because her favorite niece would be promoted if she joined. I was sure she would hold a couple of presentations and be gone. I was way off the mark. Perhaps her initial motivation was to help her niece, but it wasn't what *kept* her going. You've probably already guessed the end of this story. Sally went on to become a successful salesperson and remained one for years.

The examples are endless. After a lifetime of getting to know the top national performers, I am constantly amazed at how dramatically different they are in personality, experience, and interests. And sadly, I've worked with some bright, talented, and personable people who I would have bet would be stars. I looked away and they were gone in the blink of an eye. I've also worked with some who I was sure would fizzle out early on. Wrong again. After so many miscalls, I finally stopped guessing.

What the Masters Have in Common

If there's no profile for those who make it in sales, what *are* the common denominators? What gives any of us the courage to push ourselves out of our comfort zones and risk the embarrassment of failure? What makes us stick with something when we hit a wall? Why are we willing to do some things that are right up there with root canals on our list of favorites? Three characteristics define the winners—three musts.

The First Must: Believe in the Value of What You're Selling

Absolutely, hands down, this is where it starts. Those who succeed long-term are convinced that what they're selling is worth the price in time, money, or energy that they're asking others to pay. This belief is crucial. If a salesperson's message isn't congruent, if what's said isn't what's felt, prospects will perceive it in no time. When this happens the salesperson loses the number one persuader—the contagious enthusiasm and passion that influences others.

To a person, the hundreds of successful salespeople I know absolutely *love* what they sell. They can give glowing testimonials—and *will*, with the least encouragement! I've been at numerous sales conferences where salespeople break into thunderous applause and give standing ovations when a new product is announced. Their reaction is downright emotional. An outsider would think they had all just won the lottery.

The following story, shared at a leader's conference some years back, is a great example of the power of enthusiasm. A new salesperson from Sweden had an impressive sales performance from the start. Even though she spoke broken English and had yet to learn many of the ins and outs of selling, it didn't matter. She was an instant success. She would stand up there, hug the product, and in her charming accent, say, "I yust luf dis!" She would then go on to tell her captivated audience *why* she loved it.

So much has been written about the importance of being enthusiastic when selling, but that doesn't mean you must be a high-spirited, effervescent cheerleader type. The truth is, you can be enthusiastic with your hands tied behind your back speaking in a whisper. Others will still hear that "something extra" in your voice, the evidence of your belief.

Over time, we can forget the power of that belief. As an experiment, I proposed that, for just one week, my sales managers lock away the products they sold that they also used personally. Their reactions were instant and emotional. No way did they want to be without those products—even for just seven days. They got the message. And they were likely effusive, perhaps even scary, when they spoke with their next few customers. Most importantly, my managers were reminded of how much they believed in the value of the products and the power of showing that belief to their customers.

Just recently, this point was brought home to me once again. A dear friend called the other day. She's an outstanding sales leader and direct sales companies approach her all the time. She was considering joining a new company that had made her a tempting offer, and she wanted my feedback. Together we started making a list of pros and cons. The first question I asked her was, "Do you absolutely love the product?" I knew this talented lady wouldn't find joy in her work, no matter how attractive the proposition, unless she did. She answered yes without hesitation. The last I heard she was off to a great start with one lucky company.

It's difficult to constantly "put on a front." Those who don't love what they're selling lose an edge, that conviction in their voices that influences others to buy. Without that enthusiasm and passion, selling isn't fun, rewarding, or sustaining. Soon quitting starts sounding like a good option.

Yes, choose a company that matches your values. *Yes*, make sure that company is ethical in its dealings with its staff and sales force. But know it's also essential that you be sold, *really* sold, on the value of your product or service, because if you aren't, you're with the wrong company!

> *Enthusiasm is contagious. If you don't have it, whatever you do have is catching also.*

The Second Must: Get Motivated

> *At the moment of commitment, the universe conspires to assist you.*
>
> —JOHANN WOLFGANG VON GOETHE

Successful salespeople are highly motivated. They want success—*really* want it. Yet personal motivation is just that: personal. What motivates you may not motivate me. And what motivates me will not motivate my Aunt Minnie. And what motivates my Aunt Minnie . . . I know, I know, you get it.

These aren't just words on a page. I can easily recall many times in my life when strong personal motivation kept me going when logic said I should stop the nonsense. Here's a prime example: I had a burning desire to complete my college education, even though there was no practical reason why I needed one. I was making a top salary as a department head, and I had all the perks that went with the title. Plus, I had a long way to go to get that degree. (I had a meager eleven credits when I started.) In short, I was overwhelmed and ill prepared.

Science was tough enough, but math almost did me in. I never had the new math, which, by that time, was the "very old" math. I drove my daughter nuts asking the most basic questions. (Bless her. She would gently go over the same information again and again.) I pestered a work associate, a whiz at math, to explain what would have been a snap to others. I left class in tears more than once. A compassionate classmate took pity on me and made sure I understood the assignments.

I had other challenges as well. I was afraid to drive to evening classes because I had to take a remote road. So I purchased Safety Man, a large dummy, dressed him in my husband's work clothes, sat him on the passenger side, and off I went.

Although I was a mature, successful woman, you would never have known it by my demeanor in class. I acted like an insecure sixteen-year-old again. I fawned over the professors, asked endless questions after class, and was pathetically eager to please.

Certainly there were good times. I've always had a thirst for knowledge, and some subjects were pure joy. They opened up new worlds and prompted new thought. But much of it was a struggle. In spite of those struggles, I graduated magna cum laude.

What kept me going? I wanted to show my five grandchildren, through my example, that I believed in the value of an education. But I had another reason for wanting to get that piece of paper. (And it wasn't to frame it and hang it on the wall.) I wanted to prove to myself, and others, that I could. I didn't want to forever wonder what I might be missing. No matter how tough things were, I never lost sight of what I was working *toward*.

The key for each of us is to figure out what pushes us and sustains us. I've identified eight motivators gleaned not only from my own experiences, but also from talking to, working with, and observing hundreds of top sales performers over the years.

Look over the list and circle *your* hot buttons. Be honest. Even though you may not be consciously aware of it, these personal motivators are what get you going and keep you going!

- **Money** It's not to accumulate and count. Its value is in what it will *buy* us in tangibles or intangibles, like independence or personal power.

- **To prove we can** We need to convince ourselves and others of our abilities. I've heard more than one person say they were motivated to succeed because someone close in their life told them there was no way they could.

- **To lead or be in charge** I can quickly identify a born leader in a roundtable discussion. They can't wait to supervise others. They thrive on it.

- **Recognition** We want to know we're appreciated, respected, and valued. Recognition is a powerful driving factor and very much a human need.

- **The love of the challenge or the game** The tough or seemingly impossible is a turn-on for some people. So get out of their way and let them at it!

- **Altruism or reasons beyond self** To put a child through college, to help an aging parent or grandparent, to have a sense of purpose: not surprisingly, helping others has been called the most sustaining motivator of all.

- **Familial need** The desire to belong to a group with others who share the same interests, needs, or passion is part of our pack mentality.

- **Personal growth or fulfillment** A new adventure and feeling that we're alive, growing, and participating in the game of life recharges us, stimulates our thinking, and helps us feel young no matter what our age.

Motivation is as individual as the individual. If you're observant, it's not difficult to identify what drives others. Check out the following list. Thinking of those eight motivators, take a guess at the primary motivation for each of these people: Donald Trump,

Albert Einstein, Bob Hope, Napoleon, Julia Child, the president of the United States, Gandhi, and your best friend.

There are no right or wrong answers. And in truth, only those people themselves would know for sure. But I'd bet you nailed a couple right off.

Identifying and acknowledging your motivators is a good start. But it's just that, a start. Next, determine the end result you want. The following will take some time and thought. But please, don't go any further till you've completed the key steps in this exercise. It's that important!

Determine a specific business goal. Make it a s-t-r-e-t-c-h! Maybe it's a dollar figure. Maybe it's a title. Maybe it's the number of people you'd like to have on your team. Whatever it is, it must be a goal that's difficult, one that will take time, energy, and focus, but one that you believe, with concerted effort, is within your reach.

When you have it clear in your mind, write it down on a 3 × 5 card and put it on your refrigerator, computer, sun visor, or PDA. If it's crystal clear, put it in your desk drawer until the day it's accomplished—also known as Celebration Day! Then follow through with a simple four-step process that can make an enormous contribution toward making that goal.

1. **Write Affirmations** Now that you know what you want, imagine your goal as already accomplished. With your motivators in mind, think about specifics. Where are you? Who's with you? What are you feeling? What are you thinking? How are others responding? When you're sure you've thought of everything, write a one-sentence affirmation to remind you of each motivator that drives you toward your goal. Choose feeling words, words that evoke an emotional response. Use first person and present tense. Remember, *see it as a done deal.*

To give you some ideas, here are two of the five affirmations I wrote when I decided to write a book:

"I'm *joyful* just knowing I helped a loved one fulfill a dream." (Beyond self)

"I'm *thrilled and touched* when admirers ask for my autograph." (Recognition)

Now it's your turn. Get out your binder and start writing. Take your time. Add places and names. Rewrite or cross out and change wording as often as necessary. Keep at it until your words evoke powerful and exciting visualizations. Once you're satisfied that you've created the perfect wording, take a breather. You may think of something else, perhaps the most powerful motivator of all.

I followed my own instructions. After struggling with my first four affirmations, I slept on it. The next morning I added the final affirmation, the one that reached me to the core: "I feel a warm glow of satisfaction knowing I've written something that matters."

Once you're sure you've come up with the most effective word combinations, put them on two 5 × 7 cards. If you don't have cards handy, write them on notepaper for now. The medium doesn't matter as long as you *write them down*. Don't let me down here!

When you have your affirmations written, follow through with the next three steps.

2. **Post Your Cards** Place the cards in two locations where you will see them every day.

3. **Read Them Daily** I find I tend to focus on one or two each day.

4. Insert Feelings Interject the feelings from a previous successful outcome into your affirmations. Maybe it's an award you received. Maybe it's an accomplishment you're particularly proud of. Maybe it's the satisfaction you felt when you handled a tough challenge or crisis. Maybe it's a joyful life passage. Remember what it felt like to achieve that success, and transfer those feelings to your new goal. This step is often overlooked, but it's the step that makes the affirmations work!

These words and your corresponding feelings will keep you inspired when you hit roadblocks. They'll be a daily reminder of why you are working.

I'm assuming you're still with me up to this point, because you want to get better at what you do. So I choose to believe the cards are completed and posted. And I'm mighty proud of you for that!

When you're convinced of the value of what you're selling, and you know what motivates you to keep at it, there's one more "must" left to go, the third common denominator of successful salespeople.

The Third Must: Believe You Can

> *If you think you can, you can.*
> *If you think you can't, you're right.*
>
> —MARY KAY ASH

You know the list by heart—the many benefits of being an independent salesperson: no time clock to punch, no boss to answer to, no income ceiling, no set hours. That's the good stuff. No one could argue that these aren't impressive perks. On the other hand, employees have so-called security, a weekly paycheck, and benefits. Plus, they don't need the type of courage it takes to "make it happen" from scratch, week after week, month after month. Salespeople often hear, "I could never do what you do."

What is it that sets successful salespeople apart? The first two musts—strong belief in the value of what they're offering and personal motivation—get them going, but what *keeps* them going when the first blush of excitement wears off? The answer is simple: they must *believe* they can succeed.

> *When I took the leap, I had faith I would*
> *find a net. Instead I learned I could fly.*
> —John Calvin

Does it help to have others in our lives believe in us and cheer us on? Certainly. It's often necessary, but it's not enough. We need to believe it. Sadly, we often have habits and thoughts that get in the way of the belief in our ultimate success. I don't for one moment presume to understand the complex workings of the human mind. I *do* know, from my personal experiences, from what I've read, and from what I've observed in others, that we sabotage ourselves daily. I call these saboteurs "Gotchas." As you go through each of the seven Gotchas listed, if you find yourself saying, "Yep, that's me," circle it. (More than one circle is permitted!)

Gotcha 1: We Underestimate Ourselves I'm constantly amazed when people I admire fail to see in themselves the qualities and talent the rest of the world sees in them. Yet it's a common tendency. Perhaps it's because we're so familiar with ourselves that we take our strengths for granted and our accomplishments sometimes seem like no big deal. Perhaps it's because we've learned that humility is a virtue. Who hasn't been told, "Don't show off," "Don't brag," "Don't be conceited"?

> *Humility and confidence aren't mutually exclusive.*
> *You can be both humble and confident.*

But there's a big difference between being conceited and knowing our own value. Suppose, when you were quite young, someone sat you down and told you, in detail, what you would accomplish and overcome right up to the present time. Would you have believed it? I think not. Likely, you would have said something like, "You gotta be kidding!"

Grab your binder. Take a moment to reflect on and write down your answers to the following:

- Describe a time when you showed stick-to-itiveness.
- Describe a time when you took charge.
- Describe a time when you exhibited great courage.
- Describe a time when you were there for a friend.
- Describe two accomplishments about which you are exceptionally proud. (No, having children doesn't count. Once that process was started, it proceeded nicely on its own. But being a caring, attentive parent *does* count.)

Sometime back I attended a seminar conducted by a Jesuit priest. He talked about this specific subject. He said that we humans have a mighty short memory. When we've faced a crisis, we soon forget the personal strength it took to survive it. We tend to treat each tough time *as if it were our very first crisis*. He pointed out that if we would remember what we have handled in the past, we would know we could handle whatever happens in the present.

Gotcha 2: We Experience a Traumatic Life Event There's an old joke that asks, "How do you make God laugh?" The answer: "Tell him your plans." Or, as the lyrics to John Lennon's "Beautiful Boy" warn, "Life is what happens to you while you're busy making other plans."

A divorce, the death of a loved one, an illness, or the loss of a job are examples of events that can throw the most confident of souls. A fired executive is much more than the position he held. But try to tell him that. It's critical to remember that what happens to us is not who we are. It's one thing to be wounded; it's another to be beaten. If the pain or sadness doesn't lessen over time, then maybe it's time to shout for help!

Gotcha 3: We Indulge in Self-deprecation Suppose for a moment that a little invisible man sat on your shoulder and periodically whispered in your ear something like, "Your eyes are too close together," "Nobody likes you," "Geez, you're slow!" or "You've never been good at anything." After about an hour, you'd feel pretty crummy.

Yet, we do this to ourselves all the time. Sure, often we're a bit more subtle: "That's just not me." "There's no way I can do that." "With my luck . . ." Whatever the words, they're self-limiting. That's no problem if it doesn't get in the way of our growth. (Believing I can't skydive doesn't hold me back. I don't want to.) But if your self-talk keeps you from personal or professional growth, *then* it's a biggie!

If you tend to do this, put a rubber band on your wrist for three weeks. If you hear yourself indulging in self-deprecation, snap it as hard as you can. I promise, it will get your attention and break you of a self-limiting habit.

Gotcha 4: We Play the Comparison Game The "wholesome" lady feels diminished in the presence of the skinny girl. The balding man becomes self-conscious around the guy with a mop of hair. The high school dropout grows quiet when with college grads. The shy boy withers in the midst of outgoing classmates.

To avoid getting caught in this trap, accept that there will *always* be someone brighter, thinner, funnier, handsomer, richer, younger, and on, and on, and on. And it has *nothing* to do with your value and uniqueness as a person. (Hey, that rocket scientist might just be rather boring at a dinner party.)

Here's a tip: If you catch yourself comparing and you're coming out on the losing end, seek out the person you're comparing yourself to and tell them specifically what you admire about them. They'll feel good, and you'll feel better.

Gotcha 5: We Listen to Old, Hurtful Tapes Ah yes, the ghost of Christmases past. Past faux pas or bad experiences can influence current attitudes. A sales leader told me that in her teens she was clowning around at a family get-together, and she started singing. Her cousin turned to her and said, "Whoever told you you could sing?" The sales leader said that since that one experience she hasn't sung in front of others. I asked if her cousin had a great voice or if he was a voice coach. Laughing, she answered, "Heavens no." (*No*, I didn't ask her to sing!)

One comment, by someone unqualified to judge, influenced her behavior for thirty years. It may have held her back in a social situation, but did it hold her back career wise? No. She had no desire to sing professionally. Yet we've all heard poignant stories of children—and adults—handicapped for life because of *one* humiliating experience.

When I've allowed myself to be consumed by guilt, regret, or past negative experiences for which I can take no action, it's been enormously helpful to have a good old shouting match with myself to tell myself why my thinking is foolish, fruitless, and damaging. If you catch yourself on a similar unproductive treadmill, don't allow it to continue. Chew yourself out!

Gotcha 6: We're Overly "Outer Influenced" Outer-influenced people are strongly affected by what happens to them day to day. When things go gangbusters, they're in the penthouse. Let one or two things go wrong and they're in the cellar. It's a maddening roller-coaster ride and not a whole lotta fun. Outer-influenced people are also easily influenced by what others think or suggest. They need constant reassurance from others.

In contrast, when inner-influenced people foul up, they analyze what happened, change what can be changed, and move on. They respect people's opinions, but don't allow those opinions to dictate their behavior. They bleed and cry and hurt like everybody else. They just don't let negative experiences, circumstances, or people wipe them out.

Here are three things to keep in mind regardless of whether you're inner- or outer-influenced:

1. If you make a mistake, remember that probably the only people who never make mistakes are those who aren't doing very much in the first place.

2. If someone gives you constructive criticism, ask yourself if that person has your best interests at heart. If the answer is *yes*, consider the merit of what she said. Otherwise, as the old saying goes, consider the source.

3. When you're tempted to *offer* candid advice or opinions, follow the Buddhist principle and ask yourself the following questions: Is it kind? Is it true? Is it helpful?

Gotcha 7: We Allow Fear to Be in Control This may be the most common and most insidious Gotcha of all, because it can stop us cold in our tracks. We focus on what could go wrong (rejection is a biggie), what we might do wrong, what we don't know, what would happen if we disappointed others, and on and on. The result is that we render ourselves helpless. I asked Maria Arapakis, a psychologist, international speaker, and trainer, to give me one piece of advice she would give salespeople. She shared this gem: "One thing critical for success in sales is the ability to manage fear so that it doesn't run you. This demands self-awareness. If someone is not aware of the fears that block and demoralize them, they cannot get a handle on these fears. Successful management of fear also demands the ability to step out of a fear state by shifting focus to the worth of what is being done."

Such wise advice! If fear is making you freeze, identify it. Get it out in the clear light of day. Then remind yourself of the positive results you seek.

You gain strength, courage, and confidence
by every experience in which you really
stop to look fear in the face.

—Eleanor Roosevelt

Building a Strong Belief in Self

If the Gotchas beat us down, what builds us up? The third must-have—belief in self. If you want to grow in confidence, both in your personal and business life, you must constantly push yourself out of your comfort zone. Tattoo this under your eyelids: *All growth requires some discomfort or pain.*

To increase your belief in self, there are three things you must push yourself to do: keep learning, take risks, and learn to be comfortable in your own skin.

He is able who thinks he is able.

—Buddha

Keep Learning

It doesn't matter what it is. It can be difficult or a snap. It can take an hour or weeks. You can learn just the basics or become an expert. In your personal life, it can be programming the VCR, basket weaving, Rollerblading, bird watching, learning calligraphy, or creating a delicious omelet—whatever you want to learn to do.

Recently, I decided I wanted to learn to paint a room. I was wise. I chose a small room. I purchased all the equipment, including a commercial light that could burn a hole in the wall. (I guess I thought I would be working the late shift.) My daughter sat on the floor and lovingly and patiently led me through the process.

It took me twice as long as it would take the average bear—and I did a mediocre job. No matter; I was euphoric. I knew that from then on, if I needed to paint a room, I could. I also knew that whatever a painter charged in the future, I would gladly pay it!

Ongoing learning is critical to your business success, no matter *what* you've achieved. The following are some great ways to keep learning.

Read, Read, and Also Read! Thousands of books are published annually. Be on top of what's out there that would help you grow personally and professionally. There's no better way to increase your vocabulary than by making it a habit to look up words you don't know. (Say, parents, isn't that the advice you give your kids?)

There are many ways to find out about all kinds of wonderful books and what's happening in the world. Periodically visit a bookstore to check out what's new. Ask those whose opinions you value what they would recommend. Vary your reading. Choose periodicals that let you in on what's happening in the world around you. (Even if you skim through articles you're ahead of the game.)

> To be interesting, be interested!

There's a wealth of knowledge in books. I remember this attention-getting sign in a bookstore: "Those who don't read are no better off than those who can't read."

Sign Up for a Business Course Sign up for courses at the local community college or through adult education programs. There's nothing better to get those creative juices flowing than to be green and over your head again in a challenging subject. It shakes you out of complacency and forces you to stretch.

Listen Really listen to instructional or inspirational CDs in your car or while exercising.

Invite a Seasoned Pro to Lunch Pick out a nice restaurant, invite a seasoned pro, and pick her brain. (It goes without saying that you'll be paying.) Be prepared before you meet.

- Prepare a list of specific questions in advance. Don't ask, "How do you recruit?" Ask, "What two things would you recommend I do consistently to improve my recruiting?"
- Consider bringing a small gift to show your appreciation for her time.
- Begin the conversation by telling your guest why you admire her.

Learn Today's Technology If the computer spooks you, find a tutor—soon! Don't *allow* yourself to live in yesterday.

When I returned to school, I knew zilch about research or even how to write footnotes. And even worse, I was computer illiterate. At first I paid an exorbitant fee to have my papers typed. Fortunately, a classmate, a brilliant computer programmer, was willing to be my tutor. Since I'm a good cook and she enjoys food, it was a match made in heaven.

I was pathetically slow but my buddy was never patronizing or impatient. In my eyes she was right up there with Mother Theresa. (And I made her some scrumptious meals.)

To say I struggled is a gross understatement. I took copious notes. Every minor accomplishment was a major victory. And oh my, the goofs! Once I accidentally scrolled down and became spastic because I thought I lost all my work! I can't even imagine how handicapped I'd be today if I hadn't become computer literate. Most of my work depends on those skills.

> Hold this thought: *Anything worth doing is worth doing badly at first.*

Take Risks

We take risks every day, large and small. If you're particularly nervous about this, start small: Change the topic of conversation in a social discussion. Ask to switch one item in a set menu selection. If these are a snap for you, move on to actions that are a bit more challenging. Call someone you have allowed to intimidate you and start out with something as simple as "I've had you on my mind" or "I've been thinking about you, and ..." Speak to a friendly stranger you've connected with on a superficial level, about your product or service. Volunteer to talk to your club about your product or service.

> *Over and over I've heard "I just can't be pushy!" Believing in the value of what you're offering and being forward or "pushy" are not the same. Understand that difference!*

Be a Bit More Aggressive Don't take a no readily when asking for a business decision. Make sure you uncover the real objection. Don't stop short as soon as you feel a little uncomfortable. (You know, when you sense resistance to what you're proposing, get a queasy feeling, and begin to hear yourself sounding timid.) Point out additional benefits before giving up on a sale.

Take Risks in Your Personal Life Don't limit risk taking to your business life; take a few risks in your personal life too. If you're the beige type, paint the dining room maroon. Take a vacation with no set plans. Take a different route to work, or take an unfamiliar road just to see where it goes. Order escargot. Have the courage to express your needs. Turn down an invitation you really *don't want* to accept. Return your meal in a restaurant if it's not prepared to your liking. Ask for help if you feel you're carrying an unfair load. Follow up by stating what you want to accomplish, why you cannot accomplish it alone, and specifically what others could do to help.

> *Being assertive and being unkind are not the same. Understand that difference.*

Often we back down or choose what *seems* like an easier way because we don't want to hurt or offend. Often the result is that we end up feeling frustrated, overwhelmed, or, even worse, resentful.

Stretch I challenge you to keep changing, stretching, and moving out of the womb of the familiar so you can experience the joy and satisfaction of continued growth—both personally and professionally.

> *You may be disappointed if you fail, but*
> *you are doomed if you don't try.*
>
> —BEVERLY SILLS

Learn to Be Comfortable in Your Skin

Since the subject is confidence, I'd be remiss if I didn't mention how we feel about our bodies. We gotta learn to love 'em, warts and all. That's not always easy because of the false images we see all around us. We women are bombarded daily with images of airbrushed, youthful, emaciated bodies. Men are no better off. They too get an unrealistic message. I don't know about you, but I haven't seen many chisel-chinned, broad-shouldered, small-waisted guys in *my* lifetime. These images are *not* the real world. Don't let them sabotage how you feel about yourself! Walk tall. (Queen Latifah is an excellent example of a "real size" woman who does just that!)

Recently a beauty products manufacturer chose women right off the street who were various real-life sizes and featured them in ads wearing exercise outfits. The positive response from the public was overwhelming. We're ready to fight back.

If you truly don't like what you see in the full-length mirror, or you have concerns about your health, remember that when the discomfort of not changing becomes greater than the discomfort of changing, you'll do something about it. And perhaps some things are better accepted. I've named my thighs Ethel and Myrtle. They're my friends. I've grown fond of them.

QUICK RECAP

- Love your product or service, or you lose that edge.
- Set goals and pinpoint *why* you want to achieve those goals.
- Believe you deserve success and can achieve it. Use affirmations to stay on track.
- Identify and annihilate the Gotchas that hold you back.
- Have the courage to move out of your comfort zone.

You're highly motivated, you believe in you. You're ready to conquer the world. But is the world ready for you? The next chapter answers that question, but before then . . .

BINDER TIME

- Review those dastardly circled Gotchas. Determine what you can do that will rid you of them. Make the first small changes by tomorrow—yes, tomorrow!
- Select one thing you have wanted to learn. Take the first action toward that goal within three days. (Write down that date.)
- Choose two actions you can take *this week* that involve slight risk (one business risk, one personal risk). Be sure to record how you felt after following through with each risk.

> *Review your goals and read your affirmations daily.*

CHAPTER 2

What the World Notices: How Image Can Make or Break Your Business

We've talked about the power of personal motivation and belief in self, but what about the rest of the world? How do others perceive us? And what, within our power, makes it easier for them to like us, respect us, and want to do business with us? Let's start with authenticity.

Will the Real You Please Stand Up

Old but priceless advice: Be yourself. When there's congruity between who you are and what you show the world, others will sense that and tend to trust what you say.

One of the most powerful company presidents I knew would walk quietly to the podium, refer to his notes, pause interminably between thoughts, and speak almost in a whisper. Yet we hung on his every word. Another would run to the center of the stage, speak extemporaneously, gesture wildly, and captivate his audience. They were both being themselves.

When I headed a direct sales company, I began my weekly meetings by jumping on stage and literally screaming, "Good morning!" (without a mike). I'd challenge the audience to match my volume. They would scream back and laugh. Their upbeat response got my adrenaline going. I connected in a way that fit my outgoing personality.

A fellow distributor from New England liked my energy and decided to give my enthusiastic greeting a try. However, there was one problem—she was naturally soft-spoken and reserved. She told me her attempt to duplicate my style was an absolute disaster. She felt painfully self-conscious, and her audience sat in stunned silence. It didn't work because her team knew her as a quiet, sincere person—and an effective leader—*just the way she was.*

> *When you speak from the heart, people listen.*

Don't be concerned about how you're "coming across." If you're being real, that's the best thing you can bring to the dance. There's one more benefit to being yourself: it's far easier than trying to be someone you're not!

Perhaps you've never thought about it, but your personality, your style, and your qualities work *for* you. Take a few minutes to determine why that's so.

Zip to your binder. List five adjectives that describe your qualities or personality traits. (This is no place for modesty.) If you find yourself struggling to come up with five, ask your mother, call your best buddy, or quiz your spouse. Hold off reading any further till you've written those five. (Come on, this is gonna make you feel good.)

When you've come up with the five, jot down on the line below each how you think that trait is an asset in your business. Here are two examples.

Personality trait: I've always had an interest in people. I listen and observe.

Benefit: I think others feel valued around me, probably because they sense I'm interested in what they have to say.

Personality trait: I'm a little shy. I'd describe myself as rather quiet and low-key.

Benefit: I think others don't feel overwhelmed by my personality and tend to believe what I say.

What you say and how you say it should represent the real you. But what about when the other fellow speaks? Do you hear the real message? Are you a good listener?

Your Magnificent Ability to Listen

In our early school years we're taught how to read, write, and speak, but we're *not* taught how to listen. Yet every communication in our business and personal lives is affected by our ability (or lack of ability) to listen.

When you're good at it, you're way ahead of the game. For starters, there's no better way to help others feel respected and important than to truly hear what they have to say. Numerous books have been written on communication skills and the value of being a good listener in particular.

Years ago I took a course called Leadership Effectiveness Training (LET). It covered much on the how-to of effective listening—information that's been a huge help to me over time. You may want to check out the book of the same name. But in the meantime, here are some meaty suggestions.

Learn to Turn Off Your Agenda I know, it's much easier to say than do. It's difficult for any number of reasons. We're ready and anxiously waiting to give our opinion. We're thinking: *I can top that!* We're eager to be heard, to be validated. We're on a roll and want to keep on rolling. We're emotionally hooked, we're take-charge people, we're born problem solvers . . . For any of those reasons, we don't want to be derailed by having to listen to the other guy. We'd much rather give an opinion, solve the problem, or win an argument—immediately. Yet to be able to take the focus off yourself and absorb what another is saying is a phenomenal skill.

In fact, one of the most powerful tools for resolving differences between two people is to follow just one rule: Each *cannot* respond to what the other has said till they restate what they heard from their partner. This is known as "active listening," and it works, for both business and personal conflicts.

Whether you're talking about your product, interviewing a prospect, chatting with a friend, or handling a sticky family problem, your ability to turn off what you're thinking and really hear makes for far better communication.

So when you find yourself rarin' to jump in, pause a moment. Tell yourself, "Stop! Shut down! Focus on what she's just said. Think about what he's feeling."

Learn How to Actively Listen When understanding is vital to the discussion, active listening is the surefire way to test what you think you heard. Yet the active-listening process is often misunderstood. It's *not* parroting another's words. It's *not* a way to manipulate. It's *not* a tricky technique. It *is* taking in what you think another is thinking and feeling and then feeding it back to them in your own words.

The sole objective of active listening is understanding. If, for example, your son comes home from college complaining bitterly about the early morning classes he was forced to take because all the good class times were full, your first instinct may be to tell him how lucky he is to have the opportunity to go to college. You might suggest that he should just buckle down or that he should go to bed earlier. (If you have young adults at home, you know where *that* will get you.) Don't follow your instincts! Instead, reply with a statement that tells him you listened to what he said, such as, "You're really not a morning person, and you're feeling mighty frustrated because you're trapped by the system."

Miracles do happen. He may come up with a response to his griping—all by himself. (This was pretty much how it happened when my son was a college student.)

Here's another example. You have a business friend who is ready to quit selling. She can't find new customers, even though she's made a sincere effort. She says selling may not be her thing. Instead of immediately trying to fix it, you might say something along these lines, "You're discouraged and down because things haven't turned out the way you thought they would. You've really tried and it's frustrating that it hasn't paid off."

Listening actively to what your friend says and rephrasing lets your friend know you're empathetic, that you actually understand. She might come up with her own pep talk, but if not, you can support her with yours.

One time I was griping to a dear friend about why I was discouraged in my business. I went on and on about my problems. Poor me! When I ran out of steam, she simply said, "Sounds like you want to quit." I immediately knew that was the *last* thing I wanted to do. I stopped my whining and got back to business.

One of the glorious advantages of feeding back what you think you hear is that if you don't get it right, the speaker will straighten you out—pronto. They'll tell you exactly what they meant. That's pure gold. Think of the times you were absolutely sure you had a clear understanding of what someone said only to find out that you were way off base. It's happened to me—more times than I choose to remember.

What about the times when someone is speaking and *you're* listening, but they're interrupted by another person who needs to add their two cents' worth? When there's a break in the conversation, unless you say, "And you were saying . . . ?" the first speaker might never finish her thought. A dear friend of mine said it best: "I always encourage someone who has been cut off to finish what they were saying. But I have been left with unfinished thoughts more than once. Makes me wonder . . . was I boring? Not a good feeling." Amen.

Does active listening come easy if you haven't done it? Not hardly. Initially it can feel contrived and unnatural, but the benefits are well worth the effort. With practice you'll get downright good at it. Trust me. You'll *know* you're good when you no longer give it much conscious thought.

If you're a good listener and projecting your true self, everything should come across loud and clear, right? Almost. A lot of your message is also communicated in other ways, such as what you say, how you say it, and how you present yourself.

The You They See and Hear

When we first meet someone, we take in an enormous amount of information in a matter of seconds. That information leads us to make an immediate judgment, positive or negative. Is making a quick judgment fair? No, it's just the way it is. As you can imagine, in sales a positive impression is extremely important; it opens doors and *keeps* them open. It makes sense to do whatever we can to have that edge.

What They See

How we're dressed not only affects how others perceive us, it also influences how we feel about ourselves. If you know you look good, you'll be more confident, and feeling confident and being seen in a positive light is crucial in business situations.

Picture this: You run out early in the morning to pick up a quart of milk. You throw on some old sweats, brush your teeth, and you're out the door. You look a mess. You run into the president of your club, or your child's teacher, or a hot prospect you planned to call back, or, worst of all, an old flame. Imagine how confident you feel, how articulate you sound.

Now, let's rerun that scene. You're on the way to an early meeting and stop briefly at the market. As Billy Crystal would say, "You look *mar*-velous!" Everything works—your hair, your clothes, your makeup, etc. *Now* run into that old flame. Ah, yes, how confident you sound, how warmly you greet him!

When we know we're lookin' great, we feel great. And when we feel great, others pick up those positive vibes. I'm not a fashion expert—far from it—but I *have* learned some dos and don'ts when it comes to personal appearance.

Do

- Use a full-length mirror. Make note of what others see—front *and* back

- Know the clothing style that suits you best. (You'll never catch me in horizontal stripes.)

- Make note of those you admire for the way they dress. Any pointers you can pick up?

- Ask a good buddy for his or her candid opinion. I did. I learned that I should have the courage to wear brighter colors and that the boxy tops I wore weren't fooling anyone. They made me look heavier, *plus* rectangular.

- Buy a book on fashion dos and don'ts and follow that advice. There are lots of good ones out there.

- Consider purchasing classic resale clothing. You can have an elegant look at bargain prices.

- Clean out your closet and leave only what looks great. Give the rest away. (I don't care how much you paid or how much weight you plan to lose!)
- Remember that everything associated with you sends a message, positive or negative: your car, your products, your materials, and your display. They should all scream, "Professional here!"

Don't

- Be a slave to "what's in." (What's *in*—goes *out*.) Know what works for you. I laugh when I see those gorgeous models slinking down the runway. No way would this body work in most of those clothes! Let me change that to *any* of those clothes.
- Let the sale price of an item be the primary reason for buying it. Well-made clothing is worth the price difference. It looks good and it lasts. Buy classic designs and you're safe.
- Keep loads of clothes that don't fit. They will only depress you. Have them altered or give them to the needy.
- Wear shoes that are unpolished or have worn-down heels. An executive told me that the first thing he notices about others is their shoes. He said right or wrong, it influences his opinion about the wearer. A buddy said she realized that when she demonstrates, guests get a good look at her shoes. So she makes sure her shoes always do her justice.

What They Hear

We only deliver 7 percent of our message through our words. We deliver 38 percent through our tone and 55 percent through our body language. I've heard that statement at least a dozen times over the years. At first, I had trouble buying it. I now recognize that when someone says one thing, and everything else about them says the opposite, it's the tone and body language that deliver the *real* message.

Mark says, "I'm not nervous," but you notice a slight trembling of his hands, and he's blinking rapidly. He speaks in a voice pitched a little higher than usual. Your conclusion: Man, this guy is nervous.

Mary Beth says, "I can't believe it; Sam just broke up with me." She says it with a faint smile, and her voice sounds almost upbeat. Her hands are in an open position. Message? Good riddance, Sam!

How does this relate to selling? If you want others to believe what you say, your words, your tone, and your body language must be in sync or the listener will sense the incongruence. How do you synchronize these elements? Start by being aware of what others hear. Painful as it may be, the best way to really know how you sound is to record your voice. If you've never done this, be prepared for a shock. I thought I sounded like Sophia Loren (okay, I'm dating myself) until I recorded myself and heard Minnie Mouse. Tape yourself talking about your product or service, asking for a decision, or overcoming an objection. Do you sound confident? Do you sound credible? If you were a prospect, would you be persuaded by what you just heard?

You should also be conscious of your pitch. Women, especially, tend to speak in a higher pitch, especially when nervous or excited. (And that pitch can be terribly grating on the ear.) I'm not suggesting you should sound like John Wayne, but a deeper tone is more powerful—*and* much more pleasing to hear.

Avoid filler words—words or sounds like *umm, uhhh, you know, like I said,* etc.—like the plague. I had a habit of saying "you know" often, I mean, *really* often. My husband would stop me in mid-sentence and say, "No, I don't know. If I knew, there would be no sense in your telling me." Sometimes I wanted to strangle him, but he broke me of an annoying, distracting habit, and I'm eternally grateful—*you know*? When watching television, notice when the speaker uses filler words and how that detracts from his or her message. After a while, it's all you'll hear.

The World Notices Even More

Our demeanor and body language is part of the package. Often it's just a matter of becoming *aware* and making small changes. Here are some of the things people will notice, even if you don't.

Be Conscious of Your Posture I have a bad habit of slumping. When I catch myself, I replay an old exercise tape in my head: "Waist in. Ribs up. Shoulders back and down." Try it. It feels good, you get more oxygen into your lungs, *and* good posture communicates confidence.

Make Eye Contact Ever notice when someone has trouble looking you in the eye? What's your first impression? Mine is that the person is self-conscious or ill at ease. I was told that it's best to look in the person's left eye rather than to look in both. Presumably, looking in both eyes could be perceived as staring. I tried it for a while. By the time I figured out which was the person's left eye, they could be gone! I decided instead to take in their whole face. It works.

Make Your Handshake Count Is it firm or weak and fishlike? Today, men and women shake hands with both men and women. In business and social situations a firm handshake not only communicates friendliness, it also says, "I'm self-assured."

Honor His or Her Space Have you ever had someone stand so close that you felt uncomfortable and inched back—only to have the person move forward and catch up? Our personal space, that immediate area around us, is just that—personal. Make note of how others react when you're near them. If you're observant, you'll know if they think you're too close for *their* comfort.

Touch as Wanted Take your lead from the other person. Watch his demeanor. If you're observant you'll notice clues. I'm Italian, a born toucher, so I need to be aware that others just may not want to be hugged. Every once in a while I've sensed someone's discomfort and immediately backed off. What about those of you who aren't "born touchers" but live in a touchy world? A hug could make you feel uncomfortable, but when you know the spirit in which it was given, it's easier to cut the toucher some slack. A gentle touch back and a reserved demeanor will let others know your preferences without offending.

The Nose Knows

Have you ever been near someone who's wearing a heavy fragrance and you felt overpowered by the scent? (It's *not* a pleasant experience.) Short of leaving the room, you were trapped! Soon, you found it was all you could focus on.

Unfortunately, it's almost impossible for us to know exactly how our favorite fragrance is being received by others. (Plus, it may smell one way in the bottle and quite another way when in contact with the body.) In business situations, *always* play it safe. Choose something light and ask a candid friend or relative to check it out while you're wearing it. Then you won't unintentionally make it tough for others to be around you.

What others see, hear, and notice about you all adds up to making a positive or negative impression. By being aware and making needed changes, the world out there will be much more receptive to what you have to say. But there's one other part of you that's critical to how others respond to you: your reputation.

The Power of Your Good Name

> *What you are thunders so that I cannot*
> *hear what you say to the contrary.*
> —RALPH WALDO EMERSON

This message is short and, yes, preachy, yet it's vital to your long-term professional success: Protect your reputation as an honest, dependable person—ferociously. Of all the things about you that help others respond positively to you, *none* is as powerful as your integrity.

Think of someone you don't trust. It may be because they don't keep their word, or because they bad-mouth others, or because they've done something unethical. That person has lost the most precious of gifts—your trust. And the sad thing is, even though your opinion may be based on occasional slip-ups, a negative image sticks, as the expression goes, like white on rice.

Stuff happens. You don't meet a commitment as promised; you say something and wish you could cram each word back in your mouth; you do something you later regret. If you don't make amends immediately, you can bet others will make note of it. And over time you'll be saddled with a negative label that's mighty tough to remove.

If you buy into the critical importance of your good name, don't overpromise, bad-mouth the other guy, or make claims that aren't true. It's far better to be seen as a Goody Two-shoes rather than to be known as undependable, a gossip, or worst of all, unethical.

What's that old saying? Ah, yes: A word to the wise is sufficient.

QUICK RECAP

- Be yourself. That's the best person to bring to the party.
- Recognize the value of turning off *your* agenda and truly listening to what others are saying—and how they're saying it.
- Be aware that your dress, your voice, and your demeanor speak volumes about you. Do whatever it takes to make sure the message is a positive one.
- Above all else, do what it takes to protect your good name.

Here are some easy assignments for you.

Go through your closet and rid yourself of three items that are outdated, don't fit, or you haven't worn for months. (This includes shoes!) It's a start. Plan to do it weekly, till there's no longer an elephant in your closet!

If you don't have a full-length mirror, make purchasing one a priority this week—and yes, use it!

Be brave. Ask a respected close friend if he or she has some suggestions that could improve your appearance.

BINDER TIME

- Right before your next business appointment, review your five qualities or personality traits and how they benefit you in your business. (You might put them near your phone or on your sun visor.) Jot down how doing this affected how you felt or what you said.

- Be consciously aware of truly listening to the next person who speaks to you. Note what their tone and body language tell you about what they're feeling. Notice if your attentiveness has a positive effect on the speaker. Write down the results.

- The next time someone is speaking to you on a serious subject, take a stab at feeding back to the speaker (in your own words) what you think he's saying and feeling. Take notice if he clarifies what he meant. Write down how you felt about actively listening.

- Observe someone who's highly successful, someone who practically oozes self-confidence, and seems to attract strangers. Why do you think this is? Could part of that attraction be because of how the person is dressed, how the person sounds, connects with others, or carries him- or herself? Jot down anything you noted that you think is worth emulating.

- Set a timer for three minutes and tape yourself in a selling role. Then listen to the tape and write down what you like and don't like about what you hear—and how you can improve.

CHAPTER 3

Get Started:
What You Need to Know Right Now

Remember the question, "How do you eat an elephant?" One bite at a time. If you're new to selling, you can easily feel overwhelmed just thinking about the enormous amount of "stuff" you need to learn: ordering, company policy, promotions, ending dates, troubleshooting, etc. Remind yourself that there's much you *don't* need to know right off, and there's some information you'll need only in unique situations. Learn to ask yourself, "What do I need to know *now?*"

Once you've answered this question, determine the best source for getting answers quickly and accurately. Often, it's your leader or the service center. But before you ask, see if you can find the answer yourself in the company business manual—it's your friend. Say it:

"The company business manual is my friend!" I know, I know, the size of that baby alone can be overwhelming, but it holds a wealth of helpful and necessary information. Don't hide yours away hoping it will disappear. Check out the information, *as you need it.* Speaking of needing it . . .

Understand How You Get Paid

Absolutely, positively, no question about it, nail the compensation plan early on! Okay, maybe that's overkill, but I wanted to get your attention.

Whether you're a part-timer or going for the big bucks, it's much to your advantage to know how you're compensated for each activity in your business. Do your personal sales offer the best return? Does recruiting give you a higher percentage worth considering? What about supporting and developing others? If a leadership position is in your future, what magic number of leaders do you need to promote to attain the income you want? Have I lost you?

I know the feeling. I've seen complex-looking plans. As a consultant, I was required to learn a multilevel marketing compensation plan—a dramatic change from my longtime party plan background. (And figures *aren't* my strong suit.) Initially, I was totally lost. I asked a bucket of questions till I had it cold. If complex-looking graphs or pie charts aren't your thing, if just seeing them makes you want to get in the fetal position, just take it slowly. Read the manual. Check out the computer report or go online. Ask for help, and keep asking till you have it down pat.

There are two good reasons you should do this: (1) by understanding exactly how you make money, you'll know what you have to do to get the best return for your efforts—no matter what your goals; and (2) you'll feel confident and be articulate when explaining the business opportunity to others.

Know Your Product or Service

One of the comforting things to remember if you're just starting in sales is that no matter how little you know, you know more than your customers. That's comforting, but it's not an excuse for being casual when it comes to learning about what you sell.

All of us want to deal with knowledgeable salespeople. Sadly, they're rare. We're accustomed to "order takers," people who have little knowledge about what they're selling. We're so conditioned that we're shocked when we stumble upon salespeople who actually know what they're talking about. When you can tick off the benefits of your product or service without thinking about them and when you can answer most questions readily, you have become a wondrous exception to what customers have come to expect.

You may have joined the company because you love what you're selling, but *please,* don't let your personal experience be the sole source of your knowledge. When a customer raves about your product, NEVER let their comment slip by without asking why. This habit not only educates *you,* it makes for great testimonials.

Learn from the sales pros in your business. Ask how they persuade others to buy what they're selling. Some of their techniques may not fit your style, but you'll find some gems if you keep digging.

Be on Top of Current Information

There's nothing much more disconcerting to customers than watching a salesperson search frantically for a current flyer, or sound vague about changes or new products. I wonder about *everything* a salesperson says if he or she seems unsure, confused, or disorganized. Even small negatives can have a huge impact on customer confidence. (A friend says she's unnerved if the food tray on the airplane is broken. She starts praying that the engine received better attention.)

Do whatever it takes to be up on new product information, changes in a product or plan, and upcoming promotions. Have a fail-safe system for staying current by immediately writing down changes and appropriate dates where you *cannot* miss seeing them.

And make an effort to learn what's new or innovative in your field. If there are periodicals, newsletters, or Web sites that would help keep you on top of current trends or what's happening with your competition, check them out. How wise to be ahead of the game!

Understand What People Buy

Whether you've been in sales five weeks or five years you're probably familiar with the words *features* and *benefits*. Customers don't buy features (how the product is designed or made). They buy the benefits they'll receive because of those features. Over thirty-five years ago I remember hearing that when a man buys a quarter-inch drill bit, he isn't buying that bit to sit on his workbench; he wants a quarter-inch hole. Let's update that example: When a woman buys a little red dress, she doesn't buy it to hang in her closet . . . It's your turn, why does she *really* buy it?

Whether it's a product or service, we buy for just six reasons:

1. Because it does what we want it to do. If the salesperson points out why his or her product gets deep down into the rug and does an exceptional cleaning job, we'll not only buy that sweeper, but we'll pay more for it.

2. Because it will last. If it's a paper plate, we want it to last through the hot beans. If it's a car, we're expecting it to last for several years.

3. Because it's good value for our buck. Thus the pull of sales: We all want to feel like we got a bargain. We feel even better if we get a *steal*!

4. Because it will keep us or those we love safe, which is a powerful emotional benefit. We buy a smoke detector not just to protect our property, but also to protect our loved ones. Security is also the primary reason we buy life insurance.

5. Because it's easy to use or do. Anything that saves us time in our busy lives gets our attention. If it sounds complicated to use *or* understand, that's not a good thing!

6. Because it makes us look good to others or to ourselves, which is another powerfully emotional benefit evident in the billions spent on plastic surgery, designer clothes, luxury cars, massive homes, addresses in prestigious neighborhoods, and on and on.

Often people buy for more than one reason. Larry may buy a riding lawn mower with all the bells and whistles because he got it on sale, because it will do an excellent job, and because he can show off in front of his snooty neighbor. (You can bet the only reasons he'll mention to others are the first two.) Just remember, prospects will only buy when benefits outweigh cost, so know benefits, think benefits, and speak benefits.

Now that you're sold on the idea that prospects buy benefits, here are three suggestions to get this point across.

Know What You Want to Say and How to Say It Your training manual covers the features and benefits of your product or service, but it's vital that you feel comfortable with your wording. When you know what you want to say and how to say it, you'll sound confident and be convincing.

Here's a tip. Once you've translated features to benefits, reverse the order, stating the benefit *before* the feature. Why? Because that's what gets prospects' attention. For example, my refrigerator has a red light that indicates when I need to change the filter that purifies the water for ice cubes and the water dispenser (the feature). Were I selling the benefits of this feature, I would say something like: "You'll never have to be concerned about when to change your filter. It's a snap. The red light lets you know exactly when it's time."

For practice, choose just one feature of your product or service and determine the key benefit(s). Then reverse the order. Now sell it! Write in your binder:

Feature:

Benefits:

Reverse wording:

Okay, you get it. You know the many benefits of your product or service and how to get them across to your prospects. Now what?

Be Aware of the Benefits Your Prospects Want Most Make sure you're stressing the right (or most important) benefits by observing and/or asking a few key questions. Were I attempting to sell a car to a retired couple, if I didn't ask questions, pick up on clues, and observe reactions, I might logically stress economy and safety. They may want those benefits, but if what they really want most is the youthful thrill of driving a hot car, I'd be off base.

Help Buyers Experience the End Result Through Their Senses A dear and wonderful old pro told this story once at a sales convention, and it has stayed with me for years. She had tried many times, unsuccessfully, to convince a team member, a beautiful girl with flaming red hair, to consider becoming a manager. The company awarded light blue cars to qualifying managers—convenient to this story, but true. The pro was getting nowhere until one day she casually said these exact words: "I can just see your beautiful red hair in that blue car now."

It sounds like a shallow reason to make a career move, doesn't it? Perhaps, but it worked. At that moment, Reds began to see her hair in that blue car, too.

Let's say you demonstrate serving pieces and food items for entertaining and you give ideas for how to set a beautiful table and what to serve. You would paint the picture of your audience's busy schedules. (We're *all* busy.) You would help them *see* the spectacular spread; you would help them *feel* the ease of preparation; you would let them *hear* the oohs and aahs from their guests when they see the magnificent table and taste the delicious food.

The following is my favorite story about the power of selling benefits.

Little Jimmy was given a pet turtle for his birthday. He named it Pete. He *loved* that turtle. He carted it everywhere and kept it in his room at night. They were practically inseparable, Jimmy and Pete.

Sadly, one day Jimmy woke and saw that Pete wasn't moving. Jimmy ran crying hysterically to his father. He was inconsolable. His buddy was dead. Jimmy's dad was a compassionate man. He took his son in his arms and said:

"Jimmy, since Pete was your best friend, it's only right that we give him a proper farewell. We'll line the beautiful silver box in my desk drawer with red velvet, and we'll bury him on the hill. I'll carve a marker in the shape of a turtle so you'll always know exactly where Pete is resting.

"We'll invite all your pals and Grandma and Grandpa to attend a special Goodbye Pete Ceremony. We'll gather on the hill, hold hands, and take turns sharing what Pete has meant to each of us. Then you will tell your favorite Pete story. After the ceremony, we'll all sit under the tree and eat Mom's homemade cookies and drink your sister's fresh lemonade."

Jimmy stopped crying. He had listened with rapt attention to his dad's every word. All of a sudden, Pete raised his head. The turtle was alive! Jimmy looked shocked and said, "Quick Dad, let's kill it!"

Okay, it's a joke! But it illustrates a powerful point. When we visualize enough benefits, we buy.

This all seems logical. You may be thinking, *I know this stuff.* If you do, do you do it? It's easy to assume your prospects take the neat features of your product or service to the next step—the benefits of those features. They often don't! Spell out the benefits and help your prospects visualize themselves enjoying them. This applies whether you're selling vacuum cleaners or convincing your kids that going to the dentist pays off with a gorgeous smile.

QUICK RECAP

- Thoroughly understand your company's compensation plan for your own benefit and so you can explain it to others.

- Be knowledgeable about company polices, changes, and promotions. Have a fail-proof way to remember them. Stay informed about any new developments in your industry.

- Know the six reasons people buy and determine which to emphasize in each selling situation.

- Know the key features of your product or service and how to translate those features into benefits. Choose word combinations that are persuasive.

- Help your customers visualize the benefits they want most by involving their senses.

BINDER TIME

- What two things covered in this chapter do you know and feel confident about?

- What one change do you want to make based on what you read? When will you make that change?

- Is there anything about your company's compensation plan that's not clear?

- If so, what is the fastest, easiest way to get the information you need?
- When will you do that?
- Before your next sales presentation, single out one feature of your product or service and create new word combinations to help your customers visualize the benefits of that feature. Keep at it till you are satisfied your words are persuasive.
- In what way is your product or service superior to the competition? How will you weave that information into your sales presentation?

CHAPTER 4

The Selling Game

Those who are successful in sales always impress me. It takes persistence and skill to persuade others, often initially resistant, to do or buy something. I've learned from the best. Many make six figure incomes by getting and *staying* good at what they do. But they taught me that anything worthwhile takes work. Don't be afraid of that word! Yes, it takes effort and knowledge to reach those higher levels. But these next two chapters will help you get there sooner. Since these ideas are so critical to success in selling, as you read these chapters, put a check mark next to those suggestions that you particularly want to work on.

Remember—It's Not a Solo Act

It's an easy trap. You know what to say and how to say it. You're on a roll. Yet you can still turn potential customers off—*big time.* How? In your eagerness to win a sale you can steamroller them.

Your prospect—or in this case, your victim—may succumb (often to back down later), but it's more likely that they'll be turned off.

The person you want to persuade must be on your side. It's critical that you hear, understand, and have empathy for the other guy: his situation, his wants, and his needs. But what can you do to lower his natural initial defenses and help him become more receptive to your message?

A Key to Connecting

There's been much written and said about the value of identifying different personality styles and adjusting your style accordingly so that you can better understand and be understood. (Some companies encourage employees to take a personality profile test for this very reason.)

Other experts say that noting how others sit, stand, and gesture gives us clues about how they're feeling or responding to what we're saying. It's even been suggested that we *mirror* the body language of others.

Here's what has worked for me. By simply being observant and asking a few questions, I can usually sense which of three styles is dominant in others. Think of TBD. No, not "to be determined," but Touchy-feely, Bottom Line, or Details, Details. (You Touchy-feelys might remember them more easily if we call them Tess, Bill, and Dora.)

Touchy-feely (Tess): This is the "wanna get to know you," "warm and friendly," "build a relationship" personality style. (No surprise, this style is seen more frequently in women.) The Touchy-feelys of the world want to connect with people. They want to reach out and touch others—literally and figuratively.

My Aunt Julie is a charming, loving, empathetic, over-the-top, Touchy-feely. If I relate a story about someone, she wants to know where he said it, how he looked, how he acted, if he has kids, and if so, their names—*anything* that adds color. Invariably, if it's a sad story, she feels his pain.

Bottom Line (Bill): This is the "just give me specifics," "tell me what's in it for me," "spare me the emotions" personality style. Bill wants statistics, costs versus return, etc. He doesn't need much, or *any*, color. (No surprise, this style is seen more frequently in men.)

A Bottom Line executive friend has little patience with Touchy-feelys. He wants only the primary information—facts and figures—*minus* emotion. (The old Joe Friday style—"Just the facts, ma'am.") I can tell as soon as I've given him more information than he wants, because he starts jiggling his foot and his gaze wanders.

Details, Details (Dora): The "tell me every detail so I can cautiously analyze whether it's worth my time, energy, and money" personality style. The Doras of the world aren't big risk takers. They don't want to make a mistake, and they'll gather as much information as needed to assure they don't.

My good buddy Cecile weighs *all* factors before she makes any major decision—or for that matter, most minor decisions. It drives me crazy! (Have you ever gone shopping with a detail person? Don't expect them to buy. They're just doing research!)

> *Quick test: Without reading it again, what does TBD stand for?*

Perhaps this concept seems oversimplified, but I promise you that by being *attuned* and *aware* you can pick up on clues regarding personality style. Then, by adjusting your approach, you can help others be more open to what you say.

Let's draw from your experience. Think of three people in your life—business associates, friends, or family—who you think fit, mostly, in each of the three categories. Then, in your binder, jot down everything about their behavior that made you choose them. Once that's done, let's turn the tables; write down *your* predominant style. (If you're not sure, ask a friend or relative. You can bet they'll know!)

Someone's style doesn't always fit neatly into black and white. There are shades of gray. For example, I'm Touchy-feely (I've even teared up during sentimental commercials!) in that I'm empathetic and interested in the human side of a story—but only to a point. When it gets into too much personal detail I start feeling uncomfortable. I've learned that I also have a fair chunk of Bottom Line. I have little patience with drawn-out phone calls. (I pace constantly if it's a long conversation.) Even with *kindly* gossip, I find that after a point, I'm ready to move on. So what if you're Bill the salesperson and you're surrounded by Tess and Dora prospects? Start by making note of verbal and nonverbal clues (like my friend's leg shaking) to your prospect's predominant style, and then adjust your style accordingly. If Bill is selling to Tess, he'll need to stress more of the relationship, recognition, feeling, caring, and helping side of his proposal. If Bill's talking with Dora, he'll want to encourage her questions. (She will likely have several.) He'll want to let her know the reasons why what he's proposing is a wise, safe, and practical decision. It's the "you have everything to gain by giving it a try" kind of approach.

Several years ago, I wanted a special lady to join our training department. I knew she would be quite an asset to our team. She had a teaching degree, had been an outstanding salesperson, and was charming and intelligent. She would be that wonderful detail person we needed—knowledgeable, thorough in her approach, and cautious in her thinking. Since the prospective employee would need to move to a different climate should she accept the position, she was seriously concerned about her plants dying and how her cats would adjust. Now that's details, bless her. We allayed her fears and she joined us. And we were much the better for it!

I got an "aha" when I was writing this chapter. I realized that over the years, without giving it conscious thought, my decisions on what to wear, what image to project, and what words to use have been based on three factors: my perception of my audience's style, the occasion, and the background, position, and values of my audience.

Think about it. We want others to be receptive to us, to like us, so we all do a bit of adjusting. We act and look different at an "old buddies" reunion then we do at a meeting of business leaders. We project one image at a backyard barbecue and another at a town meeting about rezoning. But that doesn't mean you're being phony by altering your style and behavior to fit another's. Think about having a deaf, gentle, old-fashioned grandmother. You'd raise your voice—and watch your mouth!

Noting people's style can be a useful technique when you're trying to get your message across. But it's also possible to make conclusions about them that turn out to be way off base.

Prejudge—Miss the Gems

We all make judgments based on little knowledge. Sometimes we're right on, but often we're way off. And misjudging a person or situation can have anywhere from zero to major consequences.

Some time back, I was walking on a lonely stretch of beach in Florida. I noticed a tall, handsome older couple coming toward me. They weren't wearing just bathing suits; they were wearing *beach attire*. Both had impeccably groomed silver gray hair. As they came closer my instant thought was, *Hmm, rich and snooty*. I nicknamed them Mr. and Mrs. Got Rocks (GR). I guessed they owned one of the ritzy condos up the beach.

At the same time, a scary-looking *(really* scary-looking) burly guy came over the ridge of the grassy dunes. He was wearing a leather vest and carrying a helmet. His arms were completely covered with tattoos, *Hmm, Motorcycle Guy* (MG). Had I seen him on a dark, lonely street, I would have run for my life. As he came closer and began speaking with Mr. and Mrs. GR, I noticed he was cupping a baby turtle in his hand. Likely it had hatched at dawn and lost its way.

I joined the three of them. We talked briefly about the hatching season and the tiny stray. Mr. and Mrs. GR were warm and friendly, and MG held the little turtle tenderly in his cupped hand. The four of us walked together to the water's edge, where MG gently set the baby turtle into the surf.

As I continued my walk along the beach, I thought about how in the real world maybe Mr. and Mrs. GR *are* snooty, and maybe MG *is* tough and mean, but *then again, maybe they're not.*

It was a serendipitous moment and an impressive lesson for me; how easy it was for me to make an immediate judgment based on initial observations. Unlike my joyful beach experience, however, in business I've learned the downside to prejudging the hard way. I once made a misjudgment at a presentation that could have resulted in the loss of considerable business.

It was a fun-loving, responsive group. Most of the guests laughed at the appropriate places and seemed genuinely interested in what I had to say. I was *on.* One guest sat silently and never cracked a smile. Periodically she looked down and crossed her arms. Her body language said, "I don't really want to be here and I hope you shut up really soon!" I was so distracted by her behavior that I did everything I could to avoid looking at her.

As I helped guests with their order, I asked each for future business—with the exception of stone face. (By then, I was completely intimidated by her.) As I totaled her purchase she said, "I'd like to have a presentation." My immediate thought was, *You're kidding!* I didn't say it, but I bet my face showed it!

Fortunately, she approached me. She turned out to be a great repeat host. I wonder how much business I've missed because I've decided beforehand that a person is simply not approachable. Remember Sally, the lady who joined my team? I was convinced she only wanted to help her niece. I would surely have missed her had I met her under different circumstances—simply because of how Sally carried herself and spoke.

Lori Moser, a national marketing and sales training consultant, once gave a wonderful example of the risks of prejudging when recruiting. She asked the participants at one of her training sessions to share something that was true about themselves that may have made a salesperson hesitate to approach them about a business opportunity. As she went around the room she heard comments like: "I'm too busy," "I have three small children," "I don't have an obvious financial need," "I'm too quiet and reserved." Lori said the last comment was the most poignant: "I'm too old."

Does it seem logical to single out "likely" candidates—those with an obvious need, the outgoing, the quick-witted, the smart, or the accomplished? Sure, but don't stop there. Remember that the obvious is not *always* the rule when it comes to who will buy your product or service. The obvious is *seldom* the rule when it comes to who will make it in the proud profession of selling.

The next time you're in a selling situation, your mission, if you choose to accept it, is to fight your natural instincts and approach an unlikely person. You may be in for a surprise.

The Power of Your Assumptions

Is there a person alive who hasn't been warned of the risk of assuming? If you haven't heard the old saying that starts, "Never assume . . ." you won't hear the rest of the line from me. Now that you've been warned about the dangers of judging too soon, I actually want to *encourage* you to assume. Before I explain this seeming paradox, here are two stories that set the stage. I don't know if the first one is all truth or part legend that has been delightfully embellished over time. Either way, it doesn't matter, because the moral is priceless.

> Jim was an old, craggy-faced door-to-door salesman. His accomplishments were spectacular. He had a staggering

number of closes per calls. He continued to break records. No one could touch him. To find out exactly what Jim did, one bright new salesperson went with him on a call. The new kid watched Jim's every move and listened to his every word. As usual, Jim closed the sale.

On their way back to the office, the young man said, "I don't get it. Except for a few minor differences, I do exactly what you do. What's your secret?" Jim smiled and said, "Well son, maybe it's because I expect goin' in that they'll say yes."

My second story is told exactly as it happened. We received a call in the office from a lady who wanted a demonstration. I gave the lead to June, a new, enthused salesperson. June called the next day to thank me for her newest team member. I told her I was impressed that she turned a demonstration lead into a new team member. June replied, "I must have misunderstood. I thought she called because she wanted to become a salesperson. So I guess I just assumed she would say yes." I wonder how much June's assumption influenced her prospect's decision to join our company.

Never underestimate the power of your assumptions—positive or negative. When you begin a business contact feeling apprehensive, expecting resistance, or mentally ticking off what could go wrong, you're likely to get just what you expect. Then the only thing you'll gain is the satisfaction of thinking you were right. Small consolation.

When you enter each situation assuming you will have a positive outcome, you just might get what you assume. Why is that? People are suggestible; they pick up their attitudes from your attitude. Think back to a time when you found it easy to say yes to a salesperson's offer. Could you possibly have been influenced by the salesperson's air of confidence, by his or her assumption that you would?

Before your next business appointment, check out your thoughts right before you begin. Give yourself a pep talk. Picture positive results. Better yet, assume you'll have positive results.

> *Expect a yes. If you get a no, be surprised.*

Persuasion or Pressure

"I don't want to be high-pressure. I'm just not the high-pressure type." Have you heard these words? Have you said these words? It makes sense. No salesperson wants to shoot themselves in the foot by turning prospects off. And besides that, we *like* to be liked. Yet when we're overly afraid of offending, we lose sales.

So what's the solution? First, let's change the words "high pressure" and "low pressure" to "acceptable pressure" and "unacceptable pressure." No, it's not just semantics. There is such a thing as acceptable pressure. The distinction is that acceptable pressure is when the thought uppermost in your mind is how the outcome will benefit the customer. Unacceptable pressure is when the thought uppermost in your mind is strictly what's in it for you.

People know the difference. You can quickly turn others off when you're thinking solely of what you're going to get out of it. Yet you might be amazed at how long you can continue when others sense you're convinced that what you're proposing will benefit them. Does that mean you should plow ahead no matter what? Absolutely not.

Certainly, watch for any clues that your prospect seems confused or is getting uncomfortable. (That's the time to ask if they have any questions.) Listen, be empathetic, and respond to any concerns. Be attuned to when a no is really a NO! But keep in mind that what you're proposing is a good thing, and have the courage to continue to make your case.

Here's a little experiment. How persuasive would you be if

- Your son wanted to skip going to college?
- A friend wanted to start smoking again?
- Your mom didn't bother taking her medicine?

You might argue that these examples aren't fair; that those situations can't be compared to sales situations. But there *is* a connection. You would be persistent because you would be thinking of the other person. The same mindset applies in business.

Think of a time when you were considering buying something and the salesperson was persistent in attempting to persuade you to buy, yet, for some reason, you weren't turned off. Why do you think that was? Could it have been partly because you felt the salesperson sincerely believed in the product's value to you?

If you're thinking that maybe the fear of offending has held you back, consciously decide to dump that fear right before your next selling situation. Check the old high-pressure bugaboo at the door. You just might make a great sale you would have otherwise missed.

QUICK RECAP

- Be aware of three personality styles—Touchy-feelies, Bottom Line, and Details, Details—and adjust your style based on your perceptions of the prospect's style.
- Resist the tendency to prejudge. Relying on initial impressions can often cause you to draw inaccurate conclusions.
- Your initial assumptions influence your end results—positively or negatively. Go in thinking you'll get a yes.
- Unacceptable pressure is when you have only your interests in mind. Acceptable pressure is when you have your prospect's interests in mind.

BINDER TIME

We've covered much information so far. Now let's review how to make all that good stuff work for you. Please go to your binder. (This first challenge can be enlightening—*and* fun.)

- Now that you have a clear idea of the three personality styles, ask a business buddy (a natural ham) to take the role of a prospect with one of the personalities. Let your friend choose the style, and fill in the details so he or she has a clear idea of the role being played. Encourage the person to stay in character. You take the role of the salesperson. Communicate with your prospect in the way you think will best sell them on your proposition. (There should be give and take.)

  Next, it's your turn. Select a communication style not chosen. You be the prospect and ask your buddy to sell you in a way that appeals to your style

  Discuss what you both learned from the role-playing and how you would work with the personality style not chosen in either role-play.

  If you don't have a work buddy to role-play with, choose a friend or family member who matches each profile and try to convince each of them of something—what movie to see, where to eat lunch, or what outfit looks best on them.

- Think of a contact you have decided would absolutely not be interested in your proposition, and this week go back to that person with fresh eyes and a new attitude. Approach this person as though he or she is the most likely prospect in the world. Write down the results of this experience.

- Right before your next business call, tell yourself that you will be getting a yes. (Assume it's a done deal.) Think of exactly what you'll need to have ready and what you will do right after that yes to cement the decision. Write down your results and thoughts based on the experience. Did anything about your behavior change as a result of your positive assumption?

CHAPTER 5

Bringing It Home:
The Critical Close, Those Scary Objections, and Standing Out in the Crowd

Everything we've covered so far helps your prospects like you, trust you, and want to do business with you. They'll be receptive to your message, but your sales skills will be what *brings it home*. When you're skilled at closing, handling objections, and going beyond the expected, you go from playing at selling to becoming a true sales professional.

As with any learned skill, you may feel awkward at first and you may fall on your face a few times, but by sticking with it, you will get good at it. Once you have a few successes under your belt, watch out world!

The Critical Close

When it's time to ask for a decision to buy or sign on, just the thought can make your heart beat faster and your knees grow weak. Yet, unless you can close, your future in sales looks a bit dim—and that's an understatement. So let's examine this critical step closely. Asking for a decision is

- a natural part of the selling process.
- *not* an isolated event. Everything you do from the moment you say hello till you ask for the decision impacts the close—negatively or positively.
- not time dependent. It can happen in minutes or over a period of time.
- expected by the prospect.
- the part inexperienced salespeople fear most.

I was watching a show on CNN recently about top entrepreneurs and executives who take the role of mentors and work intensely, for just a few days, with struggling small business owners. These pros share their expertise and experience to help the owners become more successful.

The episode featured the owner of two dry cleaning establishments. He had a smooth-running operation with several dedicated employees and an enormous investment in state-of-the-art equipment. The owner was hardworking, smart, and open to change. He was doing well in the operations part of his business, but he needed help in the marketing area.

The mentor, along with a team of specialized experts, analyzed everything from profit margins to advertising approaches. Based on their suggestions, the owner made impressive changes.

The mentor then gave the owner a dream of a lead: a respected high-end department store was interested in his services. The potential for new business was huge—for both cleaning and alterations.

The owner made an appointment over the phone with no problem. Right before the appointment, the mentor stressed the importance of asking for the order.

In the beginning of the interview, the owner had it nailed. He was articulate and he answered every tough question confidently. It was obvious that he knew his business.

I became his at-home cheering section. I yelled, "Great!" and "Yes!" to his well-worded responses. The department store team was equally impressed. Then came the end. You guessed it—he didn't close! I started yelling at the TV: "Close! Close!"

Did he forget, or was he apprehensive about asking for a commitment? I'd guess the latter. I'm sure he went back and got it right the second time. But he could have easily wrapped it up the *first* time.

I recall a manager on my team who had a good sales and recruiting record. But I was convinced she was capable of accomplishing much more. I met with her to discuss how she might do better. We covered what she did right—and that was plenty. It just didn't make sense that she wasn't more successful.

Near the very end of the meeting, although she was embarrassed to tell me, she blurted out, "I never close." I was incredulous. This wonderful lady had been able to stay in business by the sheer power of her warmth, sincerity, and the fact that she loved the product. Customers closed for her!

My obvious next question was why? She said she felt uncomfortable closing, so she solved *that* problem by simply not doing it! The happy ending is that by practicing word choices and realizing that her prospects expected her to close, she soon became a good closer and her results reflected it.

In both cases, the fear of rejection, of hearing the dreaded no, was likely the culprit. So how do you overcome or at least minimize that fear? First, recognize that prospects expect you to close. Then, like any other part of your business, learn how to get good at it.

> *If you can't close, you're just a nice person without a sale.*

Know When to Close

I observed a sales interview in which the prospect did everything but say, "Please, please! Let me join!" But the salesperson had more benefits to cover and just kept rolling along. It was excruciating to watch. I wanted to saw a circle under her feet and let her settle down in the basement. Sadly, by not knowing when enough is enough, you can sell someone into something and then *out* of it within a short time.

So how do you know when to close? Throughout your presentation, ask questions to test the water: "Does that make sense?" "Have I explained that clearly?" "How does it sound so far?" You might even ask, "Does anything surprise you so far?" The answers will tell you if you should continue to sell benefits or ask for a decision.

Also, notice other buying signals: Listen for comments like the following: "It sounds interesting." "I wonder what so-and-so would say." "I didn't realize that." "That surprises me." "Does it come in different colors?" "What's the delivery schedule?" "Hmm, really!"

Watch body language. Are they leaning forward? Do they seem interested in your every word? Are they nodding their heads up and down? Are their bodies relaxed and open? These are all indications that the climate may be right for you to close.

Know How to Close

There's no one perfect way to close every time, so it helps to have a few word choices down pat. Your choice of which close to use should be based on three variables: (1) where you are in the interview process, (2) your perceptions of your prospect's degree of receptiveness, and (3) your comfort level.

When a carpenter picks up a tool, he'll pick up the tool most appropriate for the job. The same is true regarding the closes you would choose. The following are a few tried and true closes.

Assume It's a Yes This is the most direct close, and possibly the most underused. You simply say something that indicates you assume your prospect has decided to buy. Here are some ideas of what you may say:

- "Let's get you started . . ."
- "Let's find the best date for . . ."
- "I'll make arrangements for . . ."
- "Let's finish the paperwork and you'll be all set."

Let's go back for a minute to that CNN show. From what I observed between the owner of the dry cleaning establishment and the clients at the department store, the assumed close would have been perfect; something like, "If you have no more questions, let's get started. What pickup time works best for you?"

What made me decide that an assumed close would have been perfect for the situation? It was a hot lead, and all buying signals indicated the prospects were in a decision-making frame of mind.

Stack Up Yeses Stacking up yeses is a gentle and effective way to close because it builds on all the "agreed upon" factors in your proposal. Let's look at a hypothetical example. You have learned that your prospect, a middle-aged woman, is concerned about having enough income saved when she retires. You also learned that she shares the responsibility for the care of her elderly mother with her sister. You know by her comments that she loves the product. Her quiet agreement also tells you she thinks the amount she needs to invest initially is within reason. Here's an example of how you might summarize the positives to help the prospect see why a yes decision makes sense: "Judy, we've agreed that the extra income would give you considerable peace of mind when it's time for you to retire. And with your mom's condition, flexible hours and autonomy are a must. And we certainly know your enthusiasm for the product would be contagious. Do you have any other questions?" (You always want to allow for give and take, because you will only get to yes if the prospect has no more questions or concerns.) "Then why don't we get you started so you can take advantage of the new-host promotion."

This last touch is a key point. Whenever you can give a reason to "do it now," it makes it easier for a prospect to move the commitment from "sometime" to the immediate future. All salespeople should include a reason to "do it now," *especially* when they sense hesitancy. It can be the season, a sale, a promotion, a life event—whatever. Unless prospects have a reason to do it now, they may never do it.

> Always have a reason a prospect should "do it now."

The same close works effectively when booking a presentation. Here's an example of how you might sum up the yeses in that case. "There's so much product you'd like to have and it's great to get it for free. And some of your friends here mentioned they'd like more products. Why don't we look at dates and times that would work for you?"

Test the Water This close helps when you're not quite sure what your prospect is thinking or how near they are to making a decision. The trial close asks for an opinion, often on a minor decision, without requiring a commitment. The following are examples of questions you might ask your prospect:

- "If you were to buy, what (color, size, type, etc.) would you choose?"
- "If you were to decide to do this, how many hours would you feel comfortable investing in your business?"
- "What aspect of this business most appeals to you?"

Based on your prospect's response, you'll know whether they're ready to commit or not. All around, it's softer and less pressure on the prospect.

I remember using a trial close by asking a prospect something like, "If you were to do this, what products would you be most enthused about demonstrating?" She told me her favorites and why she loved them. I pointed out that her strong belief in the value of the products would be an enormous asset in selling; and that her enthusiasm would influence others. She agreed and decided to give it a try.

Think on this: If you find yourself using a trial close all the time, it's likely because it's easier for you to ask for an opinion, even when it's not necessary. Have the courage to use the assumed close when your instincts tell you it's a done deal.

Give a Choice Between Two Positives　If you've been in sales two weeks, you're familiar with this close. A hundred years ago the example I was given was, "Would you like Tuesday or Thursday?" It's a tried and true close. (Works with kids too: "Would you like to take out the trash or run the sweeper?")

"If I Can Show You" Close　This close can be used if your prospect has raised an objection or if you know in advance that some problem might be a roadblock. For example, let's say time is an issue. You could say, "If I could show you how to work this business around the time you *do* have, would you be interested?" If your prospect says, "Yes, I guess so," you have an advance commitment. So show her, already!

There is one absolute: know when to be quiet. Once you have asked a closing question, *please* SHUT UP! Why? You have just put the pressure on the prospect, and they need time to think about it. An interruption could throw them off. They may have been about to say yes, but you might never know if you get anxious and jump in.

To emphasize this point in a training session, I put tape over my mouth. I also illustrated how we humans just can't live with silence. I asked someone in the audience to time one minute. I then asked that everyone be completely silent till the time was up. The squirming, soft laughter, and facial expressions told me how uncomfortable the group was with silence. Just sixty seconds seemed interminable.

When you ask a closing question, press your lips tightly together and wait, no matter how long it takes. You can do it!

Now comes honesty time. Go to your friendly binder. On a scale from one to ten, one being the pits and ten being outstanding, how would you rate yourself as a closer?

If you gave yourself anything below a seven, write down why you think you scored lower. Then write down what you can do to up that score the next time you're in a selling situation.

After the Yes

So you heard that wonderful yes. Now what? Remember: prospects are most vulnerable to changing their minds shortly after they make a commitment. (There's even a name for it. It's called buyer's remorse.) Even though you likely know the following advice, I can't take a chance.

Always, always, and also *always*, whether it's a decision to join your team, host a gathering, or buy a large-ticket item, follow up in a short time with a note, a call, an e-mail, a text message, or whatever is appropriate based on what you know of the other person and your relationship with them. Your host or new team member needs and deserves your assurance that she made a wise decision.

Sylvia, a friend and top executive, offers this example, in her own words, from her training sessions:

> The "morning-after, three-minute call" was one I stressed in my training. Maybe it was because when I was new I had such a miserable record of postponements (make that cancellations!).

The morning-after, three-minute call was my secret weapon once I escaped the wrong-headed idea that if I stayed away from the phone they wouldn't cancel. (Can you imagine?) My husband's "big funny" when I let the phone keep ringing unanswered: "What's the problem? You don't have any parties left to cancel. Answer it."

You can bet, that brief next-day call often makes the difference between holding them and losing them. Your confident and quick follow-up is just what they need—*right* when they need it.

The following are a few examples of following up:

To a new team member: "Wanted to give you a quick call to tell you how happy I am that you're joining us and to see how your first call went."

Or: "This is just a quick call to first let you know what a great addition you'll be to our team and also to see who you thought of to add to your list of potential hosts."

To a new host: "Hi, just checkin' in with a quick call to let you know I'm looking forward to doing your presentation and to ask who you thought of to add to your guest list."

Or: "Just a quick call to tell you . . . (this can be anything appropriate to her upcoming event) and see how it's going with add-ons to your guest list."

Those Scary Objections

Have you ever thought, "If I just keep talking, if I don't pause to take a breath, if I make an impressive case, maybe they won't object!"

The thought of getting resistance spooks us. Just the word *objection* sounds foreboding. We picture an irate attorney vehemently making a stand in his client's defense. We see it as a battle of wits—something we'd rather avoid. But in sales, it's not that way at all.

Your prospect may be thinking, "Because of (whatever) I'd better say no," or may be wondering, "Because of (whatever), can I do this?" In the early stages, it's often because she's not quite convinced it's worth her time or money. So the quick and easy way out is to come up with a logical excuse why she can't.

Before you enthusiastically jump in to save the day, hold on! You may be valiantly attempting to solve a nonexistent problem. (In fact, it's not unusual for invited guests to think up what they'll say if approached as they're driving to the event. I know, I've done it.) Most early objections needn't be answered at all.

If your first reaction is, "*No way* can I see myself doing that," please stay with me. Let's take a hypothetical example: Mary Beth is a quiet, shy, stay-at-home artist. She fills her day with the usual household chores and relaxes by painting, reading, and walking.

A neighbor calls and invites Mary Beth to join a local book club. MB's immediate reaction is to make up an excuse as to why she can't. She says she's just too busy to squeeze another thing in. The neighbor says, "I'm sorry you can't make it, because . . ." and continues to tell MB the kinds of books the group chooses (some of MB's favorite authors) and who attends (interesting professional women MB would like to get to know). All of a sudden, MB says yes, she probably can spare some time, and is looking forward to the first get-together. Her objection was overcome when benefits outweighed cost.

At this point you may be thinking, "That sounds good, but what if it's a legitimate problem?" If it's real, it will come up again—or the prospect will raise a second objection, often the real reason.

Now you're ready and waiting. If you've been in sales more than two weeks, you not only know every objection you'll hear (there are probably only about five), but you also know exactly how to counter each. You think, for example, "Ah yes, that's number three," and you immediately jump in with a neat, well-worded response to objection number three.

Don't do it! If you come back immediately with a pat answer, you've turned it into a subtle verbal battle: She said this, so I'll hit her with this. Chances are, you'll lose. To avoid the trap, remember these two hard and fast rules when you get an objection: (1) turn off your own agenda and listen; and (2) acknowledge that you have heard the objection.

Here are just three ways to acknowledge an objection:

- If it's actually the case, say that you, or someone you know, had the same exact concern initially, and it wasn't a problem.
- Communicate your empathy. You might say something like, "I can certainly understand why that would concern you. Let's see if we can work our way around that challenge."
- Turn the problem into a question that you can answer. For example, if the objection is a time constraint, you might say, "You're wondering if you could squeeze this into your busy schedule?" If it's a money constraint, you might say, "You're concerned about how this could possibly fit in your budget?"

Remember that once you've answered an objection you must close again. You may even need to close two or three times.

What Do You Do if They Just Say No?

Your prospect has just said, "No thank you, I'm not interested," but doesn't give you a reason. You stand there feeling like a toad. Now what do you say? Duh! You have nowhere to go unless you ask why. This can be done in a variety of ways, such as in the following examples:

"Sarah, I know you would find this opportunity interesting and profitable. Would you please tell me why you think this is not for you?" By being honest and vulnerable, you will often get the candid answer you want.

"I believe so strongly in the value of_____. Would you please do me a favor and tell me why you choose not to try it? Have I missed the boat in my explanation?"

If you're new and unsure, say something like, "I know this company has a bright future. But I'm new and may not be doing this opportunity justice. Would you please tell me why you wouldn't consider it?" Or: "I truly believe it would be worth your while and fun to host a show, but I'm new. Is there anything I did or said that made you feel negative about it?"

In his excellent book, *Never Eat Alone*, Keith Ferrazzi writes, "There's one way to stand out in the professional world: Be yourself. I believe that vulnerability, yes, vulnerability, is one of the most underappreciated assets in business today."

When Is Enough Really Enough?

So you listened, acknowledged, heard, solved problems, and closed, but you still aren't getting positive outcomes. How can you tell when a no is an absolute NO? If you're sensitive to your prospects' reactions—their words, tone, and body language—you'll know.

When your instinct tells you it's definite, never allow the conversation to end on a negative note. Help the prospect feel comfortable with his or her decision. You do this by being accepting and empathetic. For example, say things like, "I can certainly understand why this isn't a good time for you" or "I can see that this could add a pressure you don't need right now."

Then end on a high note, something like, "I've enjoyed meeting you and getting to know you. If your circumstances change, I hope you'll keep me in mind." You're bound to get a positive reaction to that one, and you both go away feeling okay.

A Word About Those Noes   I've always taught that in sales we shouldn't take no personally. I've pointed out that people weren't saying no to us as people, but no to what we were proposing. However, what we understand intellectually and what we feel can be quite different. We're human. I now acknowledge that a no can hurt a little initially, so it helps to remember that it's not the end of the world, the sun will come up in the morning, and your mother still loves you.

A tip for beating those no blues: Instead of dwelling on a setback, take some positive action in your business. Call a few more prospects, touch base with a host, check in with a new team member, tackle a business chore you've been putting off, anything that gets you back in the game. It's the old getting-back-on-the-horse-again routine.

Stand Out in the Crowd

To be exceptional, do the unexpected. If you suggest a specific product that you know is the best fit for your prospect even though another choice would mean more profit for you, your prospect is bound to be impressed. That's what happened recently when my eighty-three-year-old aunt was selecting a hearing aid. The salesman didn't recommend the most expensive one, but rather the one that he believed would best fit her needs and income. She knew he had her interest at heart, and she let everyone else know too. When you suggest a product or service and keep only one thing in mind—what's best for the prospect—you will likely have a customer for life!

Here's another example of service above and beyond. I chose my current hairdresser for three reasons: she's nearby, she charges a fair price, and she does a good job. Until recently I probably wouldn't have gone out of my way to tell others about her. But I will now. She told me she had attended a beautician's symposium and learned about a new nonlathering shampoo that reputedly did an excellent job. I said I'd buy it. She suggested I try a free sample first to see if I liked it. She also advised me not to invest in the conditioner initially because the shampoo alone might give me the results I wanted. I was impressed that her sole concern was what worked for me—not making an additional sale. I'll not only be a long-term customer, I'll spread the word about her to others.

What you do after the sale matters too, though. Have you had this experience? You're in the "deciding stage" in the buying process. Perhaps it's a big financial investment and you're understandably cautious. The salesperson cannot do enough for you. He or she impresses you with attentiveness, warmth, and courtesy.

You buy, and suddenly the salesperson is nowhere in sight. Should you have a question or a need after the sale, good luck! This happened to me just recently with the purchase of a car. I waited days for a callback on an important question. (I called twice. The second time, I wasn't exactly Mary Sunshine!) When the salesman finally returned my calls he didn't even bother to apologize. Did I have nice things to say when I received a survey regarding how I felt about my buying experience? No need to answer that one. Would I buy that make again, even though I love the car? I doubt it.

How little it takes for your customers to recognize that your friendliness and thoughtfulness is not a fleeting thing that's only based on what's in it for you. Lifelong business relationships are formed by the smallest of thoughtful actions. Here are a few simple actions you can take after the sale to foster a long-term professional relationship:

- Be warm, friendly, and helpful if the buyer has questions or needs additional help.

- Send a card or brief note if you learn of a joyful (or sad) life event.

- Give exceptional service without expecting anything in return. (Going five miles out of your way to deliver a customer's last-minute gift will be long remembered.)

- Make note of and ask questions about customers' hobbies or business affiliations.

- Look for opportunities to pass on related information simply because you know it would be helpful or of interest to your customers.

These actions do take some time and attention. They also let your customers know the caliber of person you are at the core, and you just can't put a price tag on that one!

In their outstanding book, *Satisfaction*, Chris Denove and James D. Power IV divide customers into three categories: Apathetics (the merely satisfied), Advocates (true fans), and Assassins (highly dissatisfied). They state, "In order to create an advocate, a company must go beyond the expected level of service and quality to create a truly memorable customer experience." What's the benefit of creating advocates? "Advocates will tell anyone who will listen—and even some who won't—about their experience and become your best salespeople." Although the authors are talking about companies, the same principle holds true for independent salespeople like you!

As I've said many times, selling's not for sissies. It does take time, effort, and thought to become really good at selling. But the payoff is big—in personal satisfaction and financial success. Take the challenge. Look over the ideas shared in this chapter and decide what you need to learn or improve to make you stand out above the crowd.

QUICK RECAP

- The close is a natural part of the selling process. Knowing how and when to close is critical to successful selling.
- Never speak after asking a closing question.

- Don't allow objections to spook you. They too are a natural part of the selling process. Hear, acknowledge, and answer prospects' concerns to get to a yes.
- When you get a definite no, make sure to end the conversation on a positive note.
- To be exceptional, do the unexpected, and keep customers for life.

BINDER TIME

Since both chapter four and this chapter cover much of the how-to of selling, it's worth your time to linger a bit to determine what information will help you most.

- Jot down two things you have been doing right all along.
- Choose at least two suggestions you earmarked from each chapter that prompt you to want to make some immediate changes.
- What will you do differently based on those insights? When?
- Choose one additional subject you noted in either this chapter or chapter four and review it with a buddy. Compare experiences and determine what changes you each can make based on your discussion. Set a date to discuss what happened when you made those changes. Write down your conclusions.

Before we move on, let's talk about some ways we get closing experience weekly in the safest of environments. We do it all the time, whether it's persuading a friend to cut her hair, sweet-talking a partner into taking you to the movies, or convincing a child it's time to hit the books. And I'll bet you're good at it without ever being consciously aware that, yes, you're *selling*. Now, let's sell consciously.

- Jot down your answers to the following questions in your binder:

1. Think of something you want a loved one to do.
2. What benefits will you present? (Choose those that you think would be most appealing to the other person.)
3. What close will you use?
4. What objections might you get?
5. If you get objections, remember, hear, acknowledge, answer them, and close again.

Once you've made your case, think about what you learned from the experience that's transferable to your business life.

- Thinking of your customer base, is there one action you could take today that would communicate to your customers that you are interested in giving them exceptional service that goes beyond the sale? Jot it down and set a date this week to seek out one customer. Write down what you did and your customer's reaction. This one experience may stimulate your thinking to come up with other ways to be of service that may be a delightful surprise to your deserving customers.

CHAPTER 6

You're the Star of the Show: Giving Presentations

No matter what you call them—a party, a presentation, a seminar, girls' night out, a show—gatherings with a host, for the purpose of selling, have much in common. Principles that apply to one apply to all. The beauty of a group presentation is that you have the advantage of a larger audience and more potential for future business and new team members—all at once. Your audience likely consists of relatives of the host (shoo-ins), neighbors (sometimes nosy, because they're curious to see host's home), acquaintances of host, and strangers to host (somebody's buddy). A few of the guests were probably cajoled, dragged, or bribed. Some are mildly curious, and some are there because they're truly interested. And initially, you're the stranger—they're the skeptics.

Is that a gloomy picture? No, it's a realistic one. And since you know the value of what you're selling, it's an exciting challenge to your ability. Plus, you have much going for you: The host is a fan of your product or service. The guests know you're there to sell, and they're there to buy—at least *something*. The setting is friendly and informal. You have a captive audience willing to give you their time and attention. It doesn't get much better than that!

It's Your Time to Shine

Your business kit likely includes a comprehensive manual that covers everything from setting up your display to wrapping up the demonstration. Don't let the time and thought the company put into creating that information go to waste. It gives you the foundation you need. My suggestions, or reminders, are meant to help you avoid common pitfalls. They're based mostly on what I did wrong initially, or goofs I've seen when observing others.

Before the Show

Know your audience. When you plan the event with your host, make sure to do some pre-sleuthing. Get a general profile of the guests so you don't go in stone cold. You can say something to the host as simple as, "I want to cover information that will really be of interest to your guests. Can you tell me a little about those you're inviting, their age range, their interests, and so on?" The more your host tells you about the guests, the better. Are they mostly career women? Will men be attending? (And if so, what are their interests?) Do some guests have children? What special needs do they have that your product or service might fill?

During the Show

Be ready. You don't want to be fiddling with a display as guests arrive, nor do you want to seem distracted or rushed, so get there early. An equally important reason for arriving early is that it's your last chance to learn more about the guests attending. You'll want to ask what information the host thinks would be of particular interest to the guests and which guests would be receptive to hosting a future presentation.

To add to your information, pick up on what you hear and see from the moment the first guest arrives. Make note of guests' comments, conversations, and relationship with the host. Engage them in small talk. You'll pick up clues about their interests, their needs, *and* how to approach them later on a one-on-one basis.

The more you can key your presentation to the guests' needs, interests, and lifestyles, the more you will reach them. I recall sitting through a drawn-out demonstration about camping with a group whose idea of roughing it was going to the grocery store in slacks. Torture to watch! (I felt bad for the demonstrator *and* the guests.) Don't let it happen to you.

Tell the Company Story   Get guests' attention by answering the following: What's unusual or unique about the company? What impresses you the most? What establishes the company's credentials? What would be of *most* interest to the guests? Be concise when you discuss the company.

Involve Them   Involving the guests in the presentation is a biggie. You can hold their interest in a variety of ways.

- Pose a problem and solve it:
  "Have you ever found yourself . . ."
- Paint a picture:
  "Can you imagine . . ."; "Picture this . . ."; "Wouldn't it be wonderful if . . ."
- Ask for personal experiences:
  "What have you found when . . ."
- Give helpful tips. (Guests may never use them, but they love hearing them.)
- Encourage guests to touch, hold, or use your products (if feasible).

Plant Seeds for Future Business Throughout your presentation, plant seeds for future business, but don't plow, plant, and reap. I've attended presentations during which I learned little about the product and too much about why I should host a presentation or sell the product. I've also listened to seemingly endless details about gifts, trips, and the money the demonstrator has received. A little is good, a lot is not so good.

Take about thirty seconds for each sponsoring and dating bid. Arouse their curiosity and give them brief specifics. (If you're new, you might run your word choices past a critical friend.) You can personalize your offers and cover more details when you're with guests one on one. Remember, when they like you and what you say, some will be receptive to becoming hosts. When you make what you do seem interesting and easy, some will be receptive to hearing about opportunities in your company.

Know the Value of a Pause For some reason, we find it tough to live with silence—even for just a few seconds. Yet when you pause after making a key point or before introducing another thought, you add power to your message. It's also okay when you're asked a question to take a minute to form your answer. (It certainly beats using those distracting filler words or sounds.) A pause is also a subtle way to handle a distraction or the momentary loss of guests' attention.

Be Timely Your demonstration will have more impact if you tie in news that's current and relevant. For example, if you were demonstrating children's books, a current report regarding literacy or the negative effects of too much TV would be powerful stuff. Keep your eye out for those priceless gems that support the value of your product or service.

Create a Relaxed Environment

I remember a successful demonstrator who gave much of her talk sitting on the floor. Your display, your product, and your comfort level will dictate what's best for you. But whatever the specifics, keep in mind that the more relaxed and informal the setting, the better. It spreads to you and the guests.

Speaking of relaxed, guests are there to hear what you have to offer. They're also there to socialize. They want to enjoy themselves. If they laugh, joke, ask questions, or make comments, it's a good thing. Go with the flow.

That doesn't mean you can't be professional and informative. It doesn't mean you can't bring the guests back if they stray. It *does* mean that you shouldn't get locked into a script, determined to deliver it word for word no matter what. You'll get frustrated, and they'll get bored.

Lighten Up Although it was many years ago, I remember the advice I received from my friend and very first host. I wanted to shine. I read all the literature, practiced in front of the mirror, and made my family endure my "show." At the demonstration, I used note cards and made sure to cover all key points. I could hardly wait to receive bouquets.

I trapped my buddy in the kitchen. She said something like, "You did a good job, but I hope this doesn't hurt your feelings. You were so serious, so rehearsed. I hardly recognized you." I knew what she meant. I was so consumed with getting it right that I forgot to be the fun person she knew.

Learn the Power of Humor How often have you heard someone say "I'm just not funny," or "I can't tell a joke"? You may have said something similar. But at a demonstration, humor is pure gold; it can help you make a point in an entertaining way and it relaxes both you and your audience.

And even if you don't see yourself as a naturally funny person, you can make humor work for you. The solution is to be on the lookout for any humorous story or experience that will fit the point you're making. Some sources:

- A story about your family, friend, or neighbor
- Something learned from a business buddy
- Something you read or heard on television (the timelier, the better)
- A gem shared by a guest
- Something funny or embarrassing you thought or did (Others appreciate it when we can laugh at ourselves.) I still shudder when I recall my fumbled words as I introduced some top sales performers as the "cream of the crap." I shudder, but I tell it when it fits, like now.

If it flies, keep it in; if you think it's funny, but all you get is blank stares, drop it. One word of caution: be sensitive to any subject that might offend! And since you'll see some guests several times, add to your storehouse of humor regularly.

Read Your Audience   Always have your antenna up to sense if your audience is still with you. Turn, move, and make eye contact with all guests. If you're attuned to them, you'll know when they're restless. They'll cough, squirm, or seem distracted. If you're losing them, involve them, change the subject, move around, say something humorous, or pick up your pace. Do something unexpected or different by making a dramatic change in what you've been saying or doing. Think of a unique or fun way to get the group involved. When they become part of the show, they're more likely to "stay with you."

Recognize When Things Are Going Downhill Fast   It's one thing to foster a relaxed, informal atmosphere; it's another when you realize that you've completely lost control, either because the group is wound up or there are endless distractions. It's okay, on those rare occasions, to say something like, "Folks, give me just ten minutes of your attention to cover key things you'll want to know. Then you can enjoy each other's company, and I'll come around, answer questions, and help you individually. Fair?"

A Few "Don't Cha' Dares"

Without being consciously aware of it, sometimes we do little things that can create big negatives. The following are some pitfalls you will want to be keenly aware of.

Don't Get Overly Chummy As you talk with guests, keep in mind that there's a fine line between connecting and sharing too much. They want to know you have three small children. They don't want to know all their cute habits, the challenges of raising them, or your recent family trip. (The exception is when your family story is relevant to your product or service.)

Don't Knock the Competition Knocking the competition diminishes you and your message. However, if it's true that yours is the only company, product, or service that has a particular feature or benefit, shout it from the rooftops.

Don't Embarrass Your Host Don't announce loudly that your host won't receive a gift she's working for if some guests don't invite you into their home. I've heard hosts say to their guests, "Oh, please don't feel pressured," because they were uncomfortable with the demonstrator's word choices and tone. Does this mean you shouldn't make a point of the fact that the host receives more or bigger gifts if there are bookings, or that she's hoping for a particular gift? Certainly not. That would be unfair to your host and wouldn't do your business much good either. It just means be aware of what you say and how you say it. Guests should be informed and hosts should feel comfortable with how you inform them.

Don't Exhaust Your Audience I have attempted, diligently, to avoid timeworn sayings, but I couldn't resist this one: The mind can only absorb as much as the seat can endure. So true! It's easy to become so enamored with our own voice, or so eager to share everything we know that we fail to notice that our audience has figuratively left the room. Some variables influence how long you talk, like the nature of your product or service and how much guest involvement is necessary. But an old showbiz saying fits here: Leave 'em wanting more. Amen!

Don't Hang Out After You Have Finished Business They want to socialize, and you want to leave. When a host insisted I have some refreshments, I usually asked if I might take the scrumptious treats home for my husband. (The poor man rarely saw them since I usually scarfed them down in the car.)

Ending on a positive, you want guests

- To like and trust you
- To learn something interesting
- To relax and have fun
- To feel they made a wise investment of their time and money
- To do business with you again

When they do, it's a win-win-win situation: The guests are glad they came. You're glad it was a success. The host is glad she held the presentation. Speaking of the host . . .

Don't Leave the Host on Her Own The host is a key player in the success of the presentation. *Never* leave her on her own. I know from experience that this is not a good idea.

Recently, I was asked to host a home demonstration. It was easy to say yes because the demonstrator is a dear friend, plus I was enthused about the products. I also thought that the experience would give me some insights I could pass on to you. I was dead right!

Because I've had many years of sales experience, my friend assumed, understandably, that I didn't need her support. She was also concerned that I might resent her giving me advice. And candidly, I felt rather smug about my role. I didn't think I needed any help. Oh, my, was that thinking off base.

Initially, I was doing okay. I called each prospective guest, was enthusiastic about the product, and gave brief details. It went downhill from there with agonizing errors.

Because I was confident I would have a huge turnout, I never suggested to those I called that they could bring a friend. For the same reason, I ruled out inviting those who were casual acquaintances.

When a good buddy told me she couldn't attend, I felt let down. Since she's outgoing and friendly, I was counting on her to help make the event more fun.

When the second person I called gave what sounded like a bogus excuse, I was a little unnerved.

As I continued to contact others, I found that the number I was sure would attend was way too optimistic. I started to panic at the thought that I couldn't get enough people. (How embarrassing!) I also felt really bad about letting the demonstrator down. I desperately tried to think of others to invite but was concerned they might think they were afterthoughts, which they were.

After my calls, I sent out reminder invitations and figured that would do it. No "touch base" contact from me. Guess what? I found out the day before the demonstration that a relative I had counted on had forgotten the date. And another, who had said she'd be there, had something unexpected come up. I was down to three attending!

I was an unhappy camper and would have cancelled in a heartbeat if it weren't for my close relationship with the demonstrator.

The moral of the story is that date in your book is just the beginning. Never allow even the most experienced host to go it alone. Every host needs your specific instructions, your ongoing contact, and your emotional support. Follow your company's guidelines for host planning *to the letter*.

Group selling is a phenomenal way to do business. You can have excellent sales, get future business, and meet potential new team members in a relaxed, social environment. And when you know your lines, you *are* the star of the show.

QUICK RECAP

- Give a relevant presentation. Quiz your host to learn about the guests in advance. Before you begin, listen for additional clues regarding the guests' interests, needs, etc.
- Share what makes the company special. Establish their credentials. Be concise.
- Give brief recruiting and hosting bids throughout. But don't let them overshadow your product or service.
- Make your demonstration interesting by creating a relaxed atmosphere, sharing humorous stories, and including tips and current relevant news items.
- Know the value of a pause. Use it to emphasize, indicate you're changing the subject, or regain guests' attention.
- Be sure to involve the group by asking questions and encouraging comments.
- Read your audience. If you sense you're losing them, adjust accordingly.
- Don't overstay. They'll want to socialize on their own.
- Give ongoing attention and support to your host. She's a key player in the success of the demonstration. She needs and deserves your reinforcement and direction.
- A reminder: The presentation is the ideal place to find new business and meet potential new team members. You have a captive audience. The stage is set. But if you don't have your act together when it comes to overcoming objections and closing, you could end up with little or no new business. If you're shaky in either area, be sure to review chapter five.

BINDER TIME

- What parts of the presentation do you feel most comfortable doing? Why do you think that is?
- In what two areas do you want to improve?
- What do you need to do in advance to include those improvements in your next presentation?
- When will you do that?
- All improvement starts with awareness. Look over the following list and jot down your response to each. Just a simple yes or no will do. (No shades of gray here.) The ultimate goal, of course, is a perfect 10.

1. I'm comfortable meeting, greeting, and making small talk.
2. I hold guests' attention easily.
3. I regularly add new and interesting twists to my demonstration.
4. I regularly look for ways to keep my demonstration timely and up to date.
5. My demonstration flows smoothly from one subject to the next in logical order.
6. I have a high energy level. My enthusiasm for my product/service is evident to all.
7. I handle the unexpected professionally.
8. I usually replace each presentation with a minimum of one or two more.
9. I find at least two solid recruiting leads at most presentations.
10. Most of my hosts tell me they're pleased that they had a presentation.

That's a worthy list. Tackle any noes by determining three ways to turn them into yeses.

CHAPTER 7

Handling the Challenges of the Selling Game

The best of careers has its challenging aspects and selling's no exception. But by knowing how to handle these tougher parts, you're halfway through. This chapter answers three questions: How do you handle an irate customer? What do you do when your efforts aren't paying off in results? How do you get up from the "downs"?

Turning an Upset Customer Around

It happens. Sometimes a misunderstanding causes it. Sometimes it's something you did, or *didn't* do. Sometimes it's justifiable. Sometimes it's petty. Sometimes it's a company problem. Regardless of the cause, you have an upset customer on your hands and you need to handle it on the spot.

How you handle it can mean the difference between a customer who goes away content and a customer who is still unhappy and can't wait to share that unhappiness with the world. I've been one of the unhappy ones more times than I care to remember.

Over the years, I've made numerous calls to various businesses to discuss a legitimate complaint or point out an error. It's been *rare* that anyone seemed to really care that I had problems. When they did, I was almost speechless (and that's even more rare). So how do you handle upset customers and come up with a win-win?

Recently, my credit card was declined twice: once at the hardware store and again when I attempted to place an order over the phone. I was concerned, embarrassed, and in "attack mode" when I contacted my bank. I spoke with Peter Garcia. He was immediately empathetic. He apologized profusely and said he knew how embarrassing it must have been to have that happen. He said he'd check on it immediately. (I was now almost a pussycat.)

Peter came back on the phone and said he was still checking. He apologized again, this time for keeping me waiting. I thanked him for his courtesy and he replied: "Mrs. Watkins, if it weren't for customers like you I wouldn't have a job. I want to fix this for you right now." When Peter returned he explained what happened. (I had charged two items on the phone from two different states. This triggered the theft safeguard and put a hold on my credit card.).

Peter had to transfer me, but stayed on the line to make sure I was connected to the person who could fix the problem. Before he signed off he thanked me for being a customer with Bank of America. I was so impressed with how I had been treated that I asked to speak to Peter's supervisor. She said that she would write up my comments and he would be recognized for excellent service. What a pleasure (and sadly, how unusual) to be helped by someone who truly cared.

When you have an upset customer, for starters, remember that an empathetic apology is the quickest way to diffuse even a volatile situation. Let the customer know you are truly sorry that she has reason to be upset. Responses like "I'm so sorry you have been inconvenienced," "I'm sorry you have had all these problems," or "It must be frustrating, let's see if we can fix it" don't communicate that you accept the blame before checking it out. These responses *do* say that you care. A top sales leader who attended my class smacked his forehead when he realized that the first statement on his list of instructions to his staff, should his salespeople call about an error, was "Get the invoice number." When he returned home, it was the first thing he changed: number one on the list became "Express regrets."

Whatever you say, mean it. Don't allow yourself to sound like checkout-counter employees who say, "Have a nice day" in a perfunctory manner. I've often been tempted to put my face up really close to theirs and ask, "Do you *really* want me to have a nice day?"

Second, get the details. Give the customer *as much time as it takes* to "get it all out." If she pauses, wait. She may be pausing just to take a breather. Then ask questions to make sure you understand all pertinent information. If it's a lengthy problem, take notes.

Third, if it's possible, offer to fix the problem immediately. If you need more information or must check with your company, set a specific time when you will get back to the customer. Make sure to meet that commitment. If you need more time, call back when promised and set a later time.

Sometimes it's after the fact and nothing can be done. If feasible, ask the customer if there is anything she can suggest you do to help. Often, upset customers just want someone to acknowledge that they have reason to be upset.

If it's an unreasonable complaint, it'll be tough to handle it calmly and tactfully. It'll be especially difficult if you think the customer is taking advantage of you or your company. But your reputation as a professional, and your company's reputation as being fair and ethical, hangs in the balance. When you keep that in mind, you're less likely to get emotionally hooked.

When there's no way you can meet the customer's demand, think of a way you might help the complainer save face. It could be something as simple as mentioning how easy it can be to inadvertently miss or skip over warranty information. The objective is to end up with a happy customer, because you can bet that an unhappy one will be quite vocal. In their book, *Satisfaction*, Chris Denove and James D. Power IV state, "Our research shows that assassins (dissatisfied customers) are 50% more likely to tell someone about a bad experience than advocates (true fans) are to tell someone about a great experience."

There is one absolute: *Never* tolerate a personal attack or profanity. This seldom happens, but if it does, say something like, "Mrs. Jones, I want to solve the problem, but I cannot work with that kind of talk. If you want me to help, that has to stop immediately." It works.

Fortunately, petty complaints and unreasonable customers are rare. More often, the complaint is justified. Keep in mind that when you can turn an unhappy customer around, *everybody* wins—and besides, it feels good, *really* good, to know you can handle tough situations with dignity and class.

> *When you lose your cool, you lose your case.*

What Do You Do When Everything Goes Dead Wrong?

If I gathered a group together and asked them to share how they learned some of their most valuable lessons, they would likely say from a parent, a mentor, a teacher, or respected boss. They might single out a life-changing experience. But it wouldn't be long before someone would come up with something along the lines of having learned their most valuable lessons through his biggest mistakes. Others would readily agree.

We often do learn best from our missteps. That doesn't mean we welcome them. We don't say, "Yes! Bring on those glorious foul-ups!" "Say, give me more of those embarrassing moments!" or "Let me be unsuccessful, so I can reap the benefits." However, after a fall, and the inevitable downer feeling that follows, it dawns on us that though it was far from fun, we learned from it.

I've certainly learned from my down times and goofs. I've learned not to have a knee-jerk reaction and spout off during emotional situations. Waiting and thinking is far better than regretting something said in the passion of the moment. As a reminder, this sign hangs over the mirror in my bathroom:

> *Dear Lord,*
> *Please put your arm around my shoulders*
> *and your hand over my mouth.*

I've learned nighttime makes everything seem worse than it will be in the clear light of day, and that I should remind myself of that fact if I feel overwhelmed when the sun goes down.

I've learned that often if I sleep on it, I get the answer of how best to handle even really tough problems: I turn them over to a higher power.

I've learned that if I goof and find myself dwelling on what others think, I should remind myself that those "others" may not even notice, or at least won't see it as the catastrophe I think it is. They're usually more focused on how they're being perceived than they are on my faux pas.

In business, as in our personal lives, if we take a little time to analyze what went wrong, we'll learn how to handle the same situation differently in the future. When things aren't exactly going right, take the four-question quiz to make sure it becomes a learning experience.

The Four-Question Quiz: What, Why, What, When

The beauty of this quiz is that it allows you to really think through what happened and get to the *core reason* for the problem. Once you've identified that reason, you're in a much better position to solve the problem. When things have not gone as you expected, ask yourself these questions.

- What went wrong?
- Why did it happen? (Use as many "whys" as needed to get to the core problem.)
- What can I do about it?
- When will I do it?

Let's use a couple of hypothetical situations:

1. You called ten people to set up appointments and had a perfect score—you struck out ten times. You're not only feeling down on yourself, you aren't feeling exactly confident about your future in sales.

   What went wrong? I can't seem to get appointments, even after ten calls.

   Why did it go wrong? They keep coming up with reasons why they aren't interested.

   Why? I don't know how to get them to at least meet with me.

   Why? I guess I'm not strong enough to get around their reluctance.

   Why? I'm not sure what to say or how to say it when I'm caught off guard, and I don't feel confident so I probably don't sound confident.

   What can I do about it? I'd better talk to my leader and get some advice and a pep talk. I could ask my leader to listen in the next time to see what I'm doing wrong or what I'm leaving out.

When will I do it? I'll see my leader in two days. I'll tell her what's happening and ask for her help.

2. A team member rubs you the wrong way. She constantly has to be in the limelight and share her "wisdom." She steals the show and interrupts others. Last night at a meeting, she did her usual thing and cut you off in the middle of a sentence. You came back with a sarcastic remark in front of the others. Now you feel crummy because you're sure she was embarrassed.

What went wrong? I put Jane down at the meeting.

Why did I do that? Because she finally got to me.

Why? She constantly has to be the star.

Why? I guess she needs the recognition.

Why? How do I know? Okay, she probably feels insecure.

What will I do about it? I'll apologize and look for ways to give her sincere praise.

When will I do it? The next time I see her. Okay, okay. I'll apologize today. I'll even go one step further and look for the good stuff and compliment her in the future.

Getting to the core of the problem ensures you can understand and deal with it at the deepest level instead of trying to correct the symptoms of the issue. Facing up to the problem often goes a long way toward resolving it.

> *Those things that hurt, instruct.*
> —BENJAMIN FRANKLIN

You're Down—Get Up!

Sometimes it happens to the best of us. No matter what we have going for us, no matter what level of success we have reached, we hit a low and want to retreat.

Yet if you're not resilient, you won't last in business. Dogmatic? Perhaps. But it's the truth. No matter how talented you are, no matter what you do right, you'll have times when things go wrong. You hit an unexpected roadblock. You get rotten results even though you've been working hard. You're treated unfairly and feel helpless. You're facing some tough personal issues. Or you simply feel completely overwhelmed. But since you're the *sole person* in charge of giving in or going on, knowing how to handle the downs, pronto, is critical.

A dear friend, a top performer in sales for over thirty-five years, is one of the most resilient people I know. She's raised five great kids and has had phenomenal success. She's also had several personal and business setbacks. Yet she never allowed herself to stay down, and giving up was never an option. I asked her to tell me why she thought she was so resilient. She said, "I see the down times as a challenge. They keep me thinking; they keep me working; they keep me young. Early on I'd think, 'What do I do, quit and make money for somebody else? Let my kids be raised by somebody else? No way!'"

Another special lady I've had the joy of knowing and working with is the poster child for resilience. The mother of three children, she started out part-time in direct sales and quickly moved up, eventually becoming an employee of that same company. After some painful setbacks (that would have thrown most of us) and some gutsy career moves (learning a whole new company culture with each move), she's now the international leader of the direct sales division of a billion-dollar company. Talk about resilience!

In his excellent book, *Winning*, Jack Welch, the former head of GE, says resiliency is one of the key traits he looks for when considering people for top leadership positions: "I particularly liked the people who had had the wind knocked clear out of them but proved they could run even harder in the next race."

On a scale of one to ten, one being the pits and ten being the best, how would you rate yourself on resilience? If you gave yourself anything below a seven, you'll want to focus on becoming more resilient. The following are some suggestions that can help you up your score. Even you amazing tens should check out these suggestions just in case you need a shot in the arm someday. As you go through these, make note of the solutions that appeal to you so that if and when you're feeling down, you'll be ready.

Keys to Resilience

Remind yourself of where you're going. Remember why you chose direct sales and what you want to, and can, accomplish. (This is when your affirmations are priceless.)

Know a setback will make you stronger—absolutely! Think back to any difficult times you handled. Those times toughened you up. This time will too.

Ask yourself, "What can I learn from this problem?" I'll admit, from time to time, I've thought, *Please, no more education.* But I never could have accomplished what I have without those hard lessons.

See this setback as a challenge to your ability. Say to yourself, "Either this is going to get me, or I'm going to get it." This gets my juices going. My response, (swiped from old-time Westerns) is, "Them's fightin' words!"

Remember that nature has wonderful renewing powers. I walk on the beach. Hearing the waves, smelling the salt air, and watching the sandpipers scurry to beat the next wave help me renew my resolve and find solutions to problems. Both the walking and the environment do it for me. Take a good walk (or run) in the park.

Notice all the beauty around you. Instead of sitting or stewing, get moving! Solutions will follow.

Have a good laugh. Oh, the glorious power of laughter! See a funny movie, read your favorite cartoons, or find a humorous book. Laughter often puts things in perspective. If you have a pet, you're ahead of the game. They not only give you unconditional love, but their antics can make you smile, big time.

Plan a pity party and move on. I loved this idea from an old time movie star who had traveled many bumpy roads in her career: "When I'm feeling sad or sorry for myself, I set the timer for ten minutes and allow myself to be overcome with self-pity. Sometimes I bawl my head off. When the timer goes off, I say, 'Okay, what's next?'" Just in case, have you got a timer?

> *I don't measure a man's success by how high he climbs*
> *but how high he bounces when he hits bottom.*
> —GENERAL GEORGE S. PATTON

Watch Out for Those Naysayers!

When I first started in sales a friend diligently tried to persuade me that the business I chose wasn't right for me. I thought of giving up at a critical time in my career. Should this be your experience, (now or in the future), the following will help.

Look around you. Even well-meaning friends or relatives can bring us down if they constantly see the glass as half empty. Sometimes their influence is subtle, but eventually it gets to us, like water on a stone, one tiny drip at a time.

I once naively believed that a positive person could eventually pull a negative person up. Sadly, I've learned it's usually just the opposite. None of us needs this kind of ongoing influence! My first mentor said of negative people, "Love them. Bless them. Leave them."

If that's not feasible, at least minimize your contact. I once heard author Dr. Marsha Sinetar suggest we say, "I'm on a 'good news' diet for the next two weeks."

What do you do if the negative person is someone you're close to? If you truly believe that the direction you've chosen is right for you, don't let anyone rain on your parade by robbing you of your confidence or questioning your choice. Tactfully tell them how their words make you feel, and whatever their reaction, let them know that you believe in the value of what you're doing, and you intend to stick with it.

Seek out those who build and renew you. They're out there. (I bet you can think of someone right this minute.) Here's a simple test: If you feel uplifted after being with certain people, that's a big clue that they're the ones you want around you. Cherish those relationships! They'll help you go far both personally and professionally. Take a few minutes and write down their names in your binder.

If you *really* want to spread some joy, let those supportive, uplifting people know the positive role they play in your life. Send a thank-you note or call within the week. They'll feel good, and you'll feel great.

> *Problems are the cutting edge that*
> *distinguishes success from failure.*
>
> —M. Scott Peck

QUICK RECAP

- How you handle an upset customer determines whether you end up with a happy customer or one who is still dissatisfied.
- The first thing out of your mouth should be an empathetic response.

- Listen and ask questions to clarify the problem.
- Follow up promptly.
- Keep your cool.
- When things go wrong, analyze the situation by asking yourself four questions: What went wrong? Why? What can I do? When? This process not only helps you know how to solve the problem, but also how to avoid getting in the same fix in the future.
- Know how to get back up when you're down.
- Be aware of any negative people in your life. Determine the best way to minimize their influence.

BINDER TIME

- Jot down one action that was new to you concerning handling an upset customer. What can you do to make sure you remember to take that action should you be in that situation in the future?
- Think of something that's not going right in your business and write it down—come on, there must be *something*. Ask yourself the four questions, and remember to use as many "whys" as needed to get to the core problem. For example, if you are not doing well in some aspect of your business, and after a few "whys" you finally admit to yourself that it's *really* because you aren't working at it enough, acknowledge that and decide what to do and when. Be candid. Go ahead, give it a try. No one's reading what you write in your binder but you. What went wrong? Why did it go wrong? What will you do about it? When will you do it?
- If you rated yourself anything below a seven on the scale of one to ten regarding resiliency, why do you think that is? What can you do to up your score? How will you make sure to remember to do that should you hit a wall?

CHAPTER 8

Doing It All: Time Management

When you're in business for yourself, you can spend much of your day working at it and the rest of your day thinking about it. Without some structure, some direction, you can feel like you're always a day behind and running desperately to catch up. At worst, your world can become pure chaos. During these times, you're probably not much fun to live with either! So what's the solution? As your business grows, can you have it all—a business *and* a life? Read on.

It's About Time

When I thought about what I would write regarding "time" and how we spend it, I remembered a discussion I had years ago with a business associate. He said he couldn't see the value of creating a class on time planning. His theory was that if people are motivated enough to do something, they will make the time to do it.

I couldn't argue with that thinking, but I wondered at what or whose expense are they making it?

Several variables influence how we spend our time. There's no pat plan or formula that works for everybody. I'm spontaneous, easily bored, and I have a short attention span. I can switch from one task to another in a heartbeat.

Others thrive on structure, insist on order, and can be focused and productive for long periods of time. Some of us can multitask without even thinking about it. Others feel overwhelmed if they attempt to handle more than two things at a time. Some of us have several heavy-duty responsibilities; some of us have only a few. These are just a *few* of our differences.

No matter what your style or circumstances, there are ways to minimize feeling overwhelmed, being frustrated, or laying guilt on yourself. Yes, you *can* have a business *and* a life. Let's look at a few areas that can help you be in control of both.

Use Your Rhythm

I'm a morning person; I wake up ready to jump into the day, and I'm cheery, perhaps too cheery. My mother used to say, "Please don't talk to me till I've had my cup of coffee." She couldn't handle all that "sunshine" that early in the day. Others struggle to just function in the morning. They grunt their way through the first few hours. But later, watch out! They come alive and are still going strong at midnight. (In contrast, a relative calls me an "early fader.")

Some business activities can't be done based on your rhythm. You wouldn't usually make business calls at 6:00 AM or 11:00 PM. And some commitments must be planned around others' schedules. But know your peak times, and whenever possible, choose those times to focus on the tough tasks, the ones that take a clear head. It doesn't matter what the rest of the world is doing at any given time. Do what works best for you.

Avoid the Pitfalls

We're all guilty of wasting time. This isn't to say that we shouldn't take a breather; we all need recharging. It becomes a problem when we develop habits that consistently slow up or foul up our day. Following are seven common pitfalls that do just that. Circle any that hit home. (Show me a person with no circles, and I'll show you a dreamer.)

Pitfall 1: Difficulty Saying No

This is a tough one. We don't want to offend or we feel guilty turning someone down. Sometimes a request strokes our ego, so we say yes in spite of our instincts. Here are some ways to minimize getting caught in this trap.

Know what to say. If accepting is out of the question, have some tactful responses ready in advance.

- "I'm sorry, it sounds like fun, but I'm committed on that date."
- "Thank you for thinking of me. Unfortunately, it doesn't work with my schedule."
- "I appreciate that it's a worthy cause; sorry I can't help right now."
- "I wish I could make it, but this is an especially busy time. Thank you for thinking of me."

I remember asking a lovely neighbor to attend a demonstration I was hosting. Her simple reply was, "Thank you for thinking of me, but I won't be able to attend." When I asked if she wished to order something she said, "No thank you." My immediate thought was that she seemed a bit curt.

The more I thought about it, however, the more I respected her directness and confident tone. In our desire to please—or not offend—we can go overboard with explanations. This is not only unnecessary, but it also often makes you and the other person feel uncomfortable. Plus, when you extend the discussion, it can wear you down and you'll end up turning your no into a yes.

Buy yourself some time. When we're caught off guard, we can hear our mouths say yes, when our minds are screaming NO! Sometimes, we even feel resentment toward the other person because we trapped ourselves. I love this saying on one of my fridge magnets: Stress: When your gut says "No way" and your mouth says "No problem."

Often when what we agreed to sinks in, we call back with some cockamamie excuse. So before spitting out that yes, explain that you need to confirm other commitments, or you need to think it over, or you need to check with someone else; say whatever is appropriate based on the request or invitation.

When you can't satisfy a request, briefly and tactfully explain why and move on. Have the courage to say no even to a loved one. We give those we love the power to make us feel guilty. And they sometimes do so, intentionally or not. But hold firm in your decision; no guilt trips allowed! Show me the child who doesn't know his parents' hot buttons. You can't. (I'm beginning to sound like TV personality Dr. Phil. I better move on.)

Pitfall 2: Procrastination

I heard an interesting bit of information on the news the other day about stress. I always thought that things like overloaded schedules and tight deadlines were the biggest culprits regarding stress. Recent research shows that the thing that causes the most harmful stress is the constant nagging feeling concerning things left undone. As David Allen says in his book *Getting Things Done*, "As soon as you tell yourself that you need to do something, there's a part of you that thinks you should be doing that something all the time."

But who hasn't put off something because it was either distasteful or overwhelming? It's that "being human" thing again. Some of us procrastinate because we're perfectionists; if we can't do it just right, we don't do it. Some of us keep waiting for the right time. That's me. I need to accept that there will *never* be that ideal right time. Some experts theorize that it could be fear of success. Could that be you?

Whatever the reason, the problem's exacerbated by the guilt we feel when we know we should tackle something and don't. And in business, if we stall, we can lose sales. So what's the solution? These reminders may not be new to you, but as my dear father-in-law used to say when we gently told him we had already heard one of his favorite stories: "It bears repeating."

Tell yourself why what you're putting off is important. It may be even more effective to remind yourself of the negative consequences of *not* doing it. You may dread going into the garage because it's such a mess. But putting it off means you can't find what you need and you get depressed every time you open the garage door.

I know from experience. In my family, at one time the four most dreaded words when looking for something were *It's in the garage!* We were only half joking when we responded, "Let's just buy a new one!"

In business, tackling procrastination is even more critical. If you don't make those follow-up calls, if you aren't regularly out there spreading the word about your business, if you don't have an organized system for making callbacks—I could get depressed just thinking about it!

Start anywhere. I've often found that once I begin even a small part of a scary project, the thing I dreaded attacking isn't *nearly* as bad as I thought. Maybe you could start by tackling a corner of the garage. Maybe you could make calls in groups of three. Maybe you could start a better filing system by separating the first category.

Make it impossible, or at least difficult, to quit the project. This is a sneaky one. Suppose you have decided you must organize your work area. If you put everything on the floor or furniture, you'll be stuck unless you will yourself to finish. Once I emptied out everything from my bedroom closet onto my bed. I ended up sleeping on a bed loaded with stuff. But I finally finished—before the next holiday.

Make it fun. I love show tunes. I often play them when I tackle some mundane chore like folding clothes. That way, I can dance, sing, and work at the same time. It lifts my spirits. (And in my mind, just for a little while, I'm Bernadette Peters.)

When making business calls, you might write yourself some humorous or inspiring notes like, "Here I go, knockin' their socks off with my enthusiasm and confidence," or, "If Mamma could hear me now! She'd be so proud!" These kinds of fun messages work for me. I'm sure you can top mine.

Pick a spot that's uplifting or inspiring. I love nature and have done more than one "can't stall anymore" task overlooking my garden. I can hear the birds, the sound of rain, or soak in the warmth of a sunny day, and pay the electric bill at the same time. What's a pressing task you've been putting off? What's your favorite spot?

Reward yourself for getting a chore done. There's nothing much better than a sweet reward when you've finished doing something that's been hanging over your head. (No, I don't mean treating yourself to ice cream when you return from the gym.) Perhaps you've wanted to get lost in a great book. Perhaps you've been longing for a massage. Perhaps you've been thinking of buying something frivolous. Perhaps there's a favorite sporting event coming up and you'd love to be part of the screaming crowd. Do it!

What about the "I need a deadline" excuse? How many times have you heard someone say, "I work better under pressure"? Have you said it? The question is, are you saying it because you're stalling, or because your juices truly get flowing when you're facing a deadline? If you consistently find yourself in the muck and mire, you may wish to rethink that "pressure" bit.

Pitfall 3: Disorganization

This is a biggie. Clutter, either in our business or home environment, leads to wasted time, lost information, and *considerable* frustration. I don't say this smugly. I struggle with it daily.

Some of us just don't like picking up or putting away. We don't see it as a priority. It's not stimulating. It's not fun. Some of us loathe the idea of throwing anything away, especially if it has sentimental value. Or we are certain we will get around to reading those great articles in the umpteen magazines stacked in the corner. If you find yourself constantly digging through piles, if almost daily you catch yourself saying, "I know it's here somewhere," stop and regroup!

Get organization helpers. Check out stores that specialize in organizing your closet, your garage, cataloging your books, etc. You can find organizational supplies through the Internet no matter *where* you live. You also might want to check out some of the excellent books on the subject. (I have five on getting organized—I just can't find them.) Most of these books are practical and easy to follow and usually include diagrams to help make the job easier.

Check out those who are more disorganized than you. Some television reality shows help totally frustrated families clean up their overwhelming messes. Not only will you pick up great ideas from these shows, but the "before" shots will make you feel much better about yourself! (That's *my* biggest motivation for watching.)

Ask for help. If all else fails, consider doing what I did. I asked a blunt, tough (bordering mean) friend to help me. She was downright cruel. I ended up begging to keep some things. The result was a magnificently organized, clean garage, one I could be proud of. Thank you, good buddy.

If you're really overwhelmed and finances permit, consider hiring a professional organizer. They work miracles and their services free you up so you can focus your time where it really counts—on your business.

> *Remember: It's a vicious battle.*
> *If you don't get clutter, clutter will get you!*

Pitfall 4: Failure to Focus On Priorities

This is my weak spot; well, *one* of them. I mentioned I get easily distracted or bored, so I wander or drift toward things that are easier or more fun. Right now, for example, I'm enthused about what I'm writing and the dogs are giving me many clues that they desperately need to go out. (Obviously I need to change priorities pronto!)

Years ago I heard a talk by Alan Lakein, a time-planning expert. I was enormously impressed by what he had to say and immediately ran out and bought his book, *How to Get Control of Your Time and Your Life.* I still follow much of his advice. One of his gems that's been particularly helpful is the idea of making a list of "to dos" and labeling each item: A for critical tasks, B for important but not urgent tasks, or C for tasks I'll get to only if I have the time.

Anything not completed goes on the next day's list. Sometimes the Cs get kicked off the list forever. (Hey, they weren't important enough.) Thanks to Lakein, I also have a sign on my desk that reads: "What's the best use of my time right now?" This question, right there in my face, forces me to think about what I'm doing at the moment and if my time could be better spent doing something else.

Pitfall 5: Time-consuming Rituals

Think about rituals you've been holding onto in your personal life. Are they your standards or someone else's? Must your house pass the white-glove test? Do you decorate for each holiday based on Martha Stewart standards? Do you feel guilty ordering take-out or skipping recipes made from scratch because it's a family tradition to sit down to a home-cooked meal? Do you think there's a rule that says you must have an elaborate Sunday dinner?

One year, my son suggested we eat out on Thanksgiving so it would be easier on me. I jumped at the idea till I thought it over. What! No fun chaos in the kitchen, no leftovers, no bones for turkey soup, no loud family jokes? I wasn't quite ready. I may be the next time around, when I think about the energy expended for thirty minutes of eating and the mess afterwards.

Ask yourself if you're holding onto any time-consuming rituals that don't fit into your current life. If you are, be brave and dump them! It may take a little while for you (or others) to adjust to new ways—or they may never be missed.

Pitfall 6: Lack of Planning or Overplanning

Prepare for the unexpected, because it *will* happen. When you schedule a day from the minute you open your eyes till your head hits the pillow, you're begging to be overwhelmed and frustrated. Expect a business call to go longer than planned. Expect to hit traffic. Expect a meeting to go overtime. Expect to need to take a breather. If you don't build in a cushion of time, you can almost bet that the defecation will hit the oscillating mechanism.

Just as risky is not planning your day. The ABC list works. It's best to write it before you go to bed so that the next morning you're ready to focus on priorities. I once read a suggestion that a parent fill the children's cereal bowls the night before to save morning time. Somehow that struck me as a bit over the edge.

Here are some quick reminders:

- Obey the "on the way" rule. Never turn that ignition key with just one mission in mind. It's a waste of gas and precious time.
- "Waiting time" is *never* just for waiting. Keep that book you've been wanting to finish in the car. Keep cards handy. (A quick "thank you" note, written in the doctor's office, is out of the way before you know it.) Use your cell phone while standing in line, but please, out of respect for the others standing in line with you, only make brief, simple calls.

Pitfall 7: Failure to Delegate

You may be a lone soldier *now*, but as your business grows, so will your responsibilities. Be open to finding help when it's needed. How do you know when that is? When you start feeling that your business is burying you. *That's* the time to decide if some things you're doing should be done by others.

Yet many of us (especially we perfectionists) find it difficult to turn something over to someone else; something we *know* we can do quicker and better.

Yes, it's tough to watch a child take forever to do a mediocre job, but it's how they learn. Yes, it's tough to turn over routine business functions to others—knowing they may make mistakes—but they too will learn. What's *much tougher* is finding you're always playing catch-up because you're trying to do it all. Consider putting some tasks through the five-question test:

- What has to be done?
- Am I the only one who can do it?
- Must it be done perfectly?
- Does it need to be done at all?
- What part can be delegated, and to whom?

Let's talk family. If those you love aren't doing their share, speak up. Call a family powwow. Tactfully point out how your business efforts benefit everyone, with examples such as the special vacation the family took, the larger home you were able to afford, the college tuitions you can help pay for, etc. A "we're all in this together" approach will work best.

Without recriminations, spell out what you need from others and why. Brainstorm compromises. Make sure accountability is built into agreed-upon commitments. If a spouse agrees to help with paperwork, if a child volunteers to organize your materials, then hold them to it. If you don't you'll be right back where you started, on overload.

Beware: You never want to become a simmering volcano. By not voicing your wishes, you'll build up a lot of resentment. You'll get rid of it all right; you'll finally erupt over some petty thing to everyone's shocked amazement.

And don't book any guilt trips. When you know you're doing the best you can with the time you have, don't allow yourself to feel guilty if others aren't exactly joyful with your decisions. You'll never please them all. I love this comment passed on by my friend: "It wasn't my children; it was always my stay-at-home mother who could really lay the guilt on me. When I heard the following, I thought, My mother would have loved to use that one!"

> Mother: "I haven't eaten in days."
>
> Daughter: "Why, Mom?"
>
> Mother: "I didn't want to have my mouth full
>   in case you called."

As you read through this section, I know you found yourself nodding your head up and down when some things hit close to home. Don't let those insights go to waste. Promise yourself that *this* is the year for change. How freeing it will be to take control of areas that have been controlling you.

Thank You, Alexander Graham Bell: Time and the Telephone

Ah yes, the telephone, that wonderful convenience. It's both our friend and our enemy. We couldn't imagine life without it. In mere minutes we can connect with a loved one half a world away! And in business, it's indispensable. But knowing how to make the phone work *best* for you is key. And that means controlling your time on the phone through technology and a few practical strategies.

Technology

Telephone technology today is far removed from simply dialing a few numbers and reaching Aunt Minnie. The many features now available can simplify our lives, make for peaceful dinners, and tell us who called in our absence. They can screen our calls. They can protect us and cover for us day and night. How wonderful! But those same conveniences can also be mighty irritating to hapless callers, and if you don't watch it, they can harm your business.

Voice Mail This is one of the best things to happen to businesspeople. You have the comfort of knowing that when you're away from home you'll never miss an important call. Just make sure it works *for* you, instead of *against* you. Ask yourself these four questions:

1. **Is my message clear and professional?** In the desire to cover it all, I've heard a multitude of jumbled choices: a sales pitch, both for customers and the sales team; a business promotion; and a thought for the day.

   I may be stepping on some toes, but is it possible you're making that little machine do far too much work and confusing, or possibly even irritating, those who call? The message represents *you*. Question whether it does a good job. If you're not sure, remind yourself that the primary reasons for voice mail are to let you know who needs or wants to speak to you, and how to contact them and when.

2. **Is my message current?** Jane's voice mail says she's on vacation till a specific date. I'm calling four days after her supposed return. Where in the world are you, Jane? Not good PR.

3. **Do I check my messages regularly?** There's nothing more frustrating than being told by a machine that someone will get back to you soon, and then not hearing from them for days. It makes the caller feel insignificant and gives the impression that you're disorganized, or worse yet, disinterested. Your "call back" promise on the phone is just as binding as giving your word in person.

Sadly, this may be one of the common reasons salespeople lose potential customers. It's happened to me. After a few days of waiting for a representative to call, I bought the product from a competitor. After some time had passed and the service I was interested in didn't return my call, I contacted someone else.

4. **Do I overuse voice mail?** It can be easy to have that baby on for hours every day. What freedom! The downside is that callers won't be thrilled. I get frustrated when I get a machine almost every time I call. When I finally reach a human being, I've been known to say: "Is that really you? Hallelujah!" Potential customers or prospective team members may think that you're not that interested in them or their business. Ouch!

What About Leaving a Message?

More times than I care to remember, someone has left a message and garbled their name so that I had no idea who was calling, or rattled off their number so quickly that it was unintelligible and I had no way to contact them. When leaving a message, emphasize your name, speak slowly, and repeat your telephone number twice, with the area code.

Call Waiting Here's my subjective opinion: I hate it. I think it is the rudest device ever created. No call is so important that it should be given the power to interrupt another call. If it's an emergency, the operator will interrupt. If you're waiting for a crucial call, tell the person on the line you'll call back after you receive that call. (I guess there's no question about how I feel about call waiting?)

Another way to let others know when you're there but temporarily tied up is to use a voice mail service through the telephone company. When I'm using the phone and someone calls, a message tells the caller that I'm on the phone and that I'll return his or her call as soon as possible. Just make sure to check for messages after you hang up.

Caller ID This is a practical and wise investment. It not only buys you time if you can't or don't want to talk to the caller right then; it also protects you from unwanted or threatening calls. Just one reminder: eventually call those you choose to hold off, unless you want them out of your life forever. Poor Aunt Minnie; she's still waiting. And that name you couldn't identify? It just might have been a hot lead!

Controlling Phone Time

Aside from the problems phone technology can present, there's no ignoring that simply letting the time you spend on the phone get out of control can be a major misuse of time. Here are some suggestions to help control phone time.

Know What You Want to Say If you're calling a business prospect or talking to a team member regarding a sensitive or involved subject, write yourself a brief script so you sound assured and stay on track.

Keep to the Subject If you tend to wander, be aware of when you start going off on a tangent and get back to the purpose of the call. (You might write yourself a threatening note and keep it in front of you.)

If others wander, tactfully tell them you need to focus on the purpose of your call: "I'd love to hear more about your new furniture, Mary Beth, but I know you're busy, and I have just a brief time to tell you . . ."

If you know in advance that you're calling someone who tends to go on and on, set the parameters up front: "I have just five minutes, Jane, but wanted to let you to know . . ."

Use a Timer You may be amazed at how much time you can chew up on what *started out* to be a simple five-minute call. That ticking makes you aware.

Know How to Exit Tactfully Let those who call you know if you are in the middle of something or have only a brief time to talk. You might ask if you may call back. I have had people tell me, after several minutes, that they really had to go because of a pressing need. I ended up feeling rotten because I had held them up.

But what about Aunt Minnie? We all have a friend or family member who loves to chat. They can go on and on. We're chewing our nails wondering how we'll ever get our work done—and the caller is blissfully unaware. Tactful honesty sure beats halfhearted listening or quiet frustration any day. If this happens to you often, perhaps it's time to let those close to you know the hours you're likely to be tied up. Or you could set aside some time on a regular basis to touch base with those you love.

Balance, Glorious Balance

We all want balance in our lives. None of us likes the idea of being consumed by one area of life at the expense of other areas. Experts have pounded this point to death. Yet is fair and even distribution of our time always realistic?

I attended a creative thinking seminar at a crucial time in my career. At one point the instructor listed six human needs. If we identified any areas that we were shortchanging, we were to think creatively about what we could do about it. The six needs were

(1) financial, (2) spiritual, (3) physical, (4) familial, (5) social, and (6) intellectual.

My first reaction was, "Holy cow, I'm not doing justice to *any* of these!" My second reaction was the realization that my business was consuming more of my time than other needs, which led to guilt, guilt, and more guilt. I eventually accepted that there was no way I could—or wanted to—give equal time to each area. I concluded that I had to do the following:

- Be realistic and recognize my time couldn't always be divided evenly
- Accept that my business would often take a large chunk of time
- Determine current priorities and divide my time accordingly
- Recognize that personal or family needs or events would sometimes take precedent—no matter what my business commitments
- Realize that I wasn't Superwoman
- Resist trying to please everybody or going by someone else's rules

I decided that as long as no need was completely neglected, I was doing okay. Over time, circumstances and our priorities change, and so does the time we spend on any of the six needs, and that's okay, too.

Review the six priorities list. Think of how you fill your day, your week, and your month. Ask yourself the following questions: Are there areas that deserve a bit more of my time? Are there any that could receive less? Are there some I could combine?

Once you're satisfied that this is the best you can do at this time in your life, don't let the rest of the world make you feel not okay!

Finally, remember: When you're constantly giving to others—caring, listening, helping, doing—it gets mighty easy to forget to "fill the well." The risk is that the well will run dry. The toughest thing for highly motivated people to do is to learn to "turn it off." Remember to take time for you. What gives you pleasure? What makes you laugh? What transports you to a quiet, peaceful place in mind or body? Take the time to go there.

Stephanie Culp, author and time management expert, summed this up beautifully: "Each moment of your life, once spent, is gone forever. Live your life with that in mind and learn to make each moment count."

QUICK RECAP

- Know your peak hours and use them for the more challenging tasks
- Take a midday break to refresh your mind and body
- Be aware of the seven pitfalls: (1) difficulty saying no, (2) procrastination, (3) disorganization, (4) failure to focus on priorities, (5) lack of planning or overplanning, (6) time-consuming rituals, and (7) failure to delegate.
- Examine the way you use the phone in business, and make sure you're using that time well.
- Know the six human needs so you can determine how to best divide your time to fill each: (1) financial, (2) spiritual, (3) physical, (4) familial, (5) social, and (6) intellectual.

BINDER TIME

- Write down two things you're handling well regarding the use of your time.

- Ask yourself if you're using your "peak times" to tackle your most challenging tasks. If not, write down one change you'll make in your schedule this week.
- Find a quiet spot, preferably around 1:30 PM. Relax and focus entirely on your breathing. Jot down the effects.
- Review the pitfalls you circled. Decide on two small changes you can make immediately in each area that will free up more time.
- Thinking of how you've been using phone technology, what one change would result in your putting it to better use? When will you make that change?
- Thinking of the six needs, are there any you're shortchanging? If yes, do you have any solutions? Think of a realistic option to address any neglected need within the next week. If, for example, you recognize that you haven't been in touch with a dear friend in several weeks, make that phone call and catch up. (If time permits, consider a luncheon date. You need to eat anyway. What a great way to enjoy it more.)
- Pick one big project or behavior that's really getting in the way of using your time wisely. Make a small change immediately and jot down the date. Take one action each week over the next month and note it in your binder. At the end of the month you will have reached your goal of using your time more wisely. Once you have, pat yourself on the back and treat yourself to a small reward.

CHAPTER 9

Staying in the Game

It's one thing to *start* a direct sales business with the help of friends, relatives, and willing acquaintances, but it's quite another to stay in business. You do that by being prepared, being seen, and speaking up. This is the time when the committed stand out. Is it scary? Sure, but it's the best way to grow in the sales profession. I remember clearly that my confidence increased considerably with that shift. Why? I recognized that once I succeeded in getting business completely on my own, no one could ever take that away from me. I then had the comforting knowledge that I did it once and I could do it again! (I also remember being less sensitive to a no when it came from strangers rather than family and friends.) So, how can you reach the outside world?

Be Aware, They're Everywhere

Prospective business contacts are all around you. They're at business functions, club meetings, athletic events, checkout lines, charitable events, church, social gatherings, on the street, in the park, and around the corner.

Wouldn't it be great if they had check marks on their foreheads, or if a voice within us whispered, "Over there!" No such luck, but by being attuned to your surroundings, you'll find them. It starts with awareness. We see what we educate ourselves to see; we hear what we educate ourselves to hear. Here are a few examples to illustrate my point further.

I'd taken the same route to work for years, but with the exception of the stoplights and crossroads, I was oblivious to what was around me. One day I took a close look at a home at an intersection I crossed every day. Had I been shown a picture of that home the night before, there's no way I could have identified its location. It wasn't important to me. I was focused on getting to work on time.

I stopped typing the other day and sat quietly for a moment. I became acutely aware of the low hum of the computer. It was there all the time, but I was absorbed in my thoughts and never heard it. It wasn't important to me and I tuned it out. Had I paid attention, the steady noise would have been an annoying distraction.

Neither of those observations would have been helpful to me. But what might I miss if I didn't make a conscious effort to make note of clues that could open doors in my business?

By now you may be thinking, "I get it. I'm aware that I should be aware; but be more specific." Okay, let's say you're at a business or social gathering. Notice, seek out, and start a conversation with the following people: the friendly person, the popular person, the obvious leader, and the funny person. You should also approach the loner, who may be the very person who will be most receptive to your friendly greeting. If it's a social gathering, it's likely not appropriate to launch into business, but it's okay to get contact information for a later follow-up.

Please take just a minute, right now, to jot down three more types of people to approach, considering what you sell.

Now that we've talked about approachable types, what does it take to reach them?

Be Ready Have business cards with you at all times, along with professionally packaged information. If applicable, keep new samples in your car. When out and about, consider wearing a professional-looking nametag, and if feasible, a tote with your company logo. (Then don't be surprised if someone approaches *you*.)

Be Out There Increase your chances of finding your next customer or team member by creating opportunities to meet more people. Ask yourself these three questions:

1. Is there a professional group I should join?
2. Is there a social club I might consider?
3. Is there a volunteer organization I could help?

The more you see and the more you're seen, the better.

Be Approachable You've heard this song before: smile, make eye contact, and have open body language. Speaking of the body, does yours shout "confident"? I remember that old exercise routine: stomach in, ribs up, and shoulders back and down. (You know, the stance you guys take when you see a beautiful woman approaching.)

Learn the Art of Small Talk How comforting to have something of interest to say when you meet someone new. How wonderful to walk into a room full of strangers and be able to start up a conversation with ease. If it's not one of your strengths, it can be learned. It just takes a little practice. Yes, you can strike up a conversation about the weather or sports, but as George Burns said when asked how he felt about dying, "It's been done before."

Give a personal opinion, share a frustration, talk about a recent funny or embarrassing experience, anything that makes you real and interesting.

At a conference, I struck up a conversation with a friendly face. He was obviously a regular conference attendee. His first comment was, "If I eat one more rubber chicken, I'll puke!" A bit crude perhaps, but he was being himself. We were on common ground. We laughed and took it from there.

I was in the grocery store late in the day (in the supposed *fast* lane), and the person ahead of me needed a credit that only the manager could approve. I waited for what seemed an interminable amount of time. I turned to the woman behind me and said, "I'm tired and grumpy; I don't want to be patient. I'm all out of 'nice'!" She said she felt the same. We laughed, chatted, and never thought more about waiting. We had shared a real moment. When you learn the art of small talk, you open the door to connecting with others. Once you connect, it's much easier to talk about your business.

Be Truly Interested Turn off your own agenda and tune in to people you meet. Most of us get way too little sincere attention from others. When it happens, it's a pleasant surprise. Ask open-ended questions like the following:

- "What do you find the most frustrating?"
- "What gives you the biggest kick?"
- "What is the most interesting aspect of . . .?"
- "What drew you to . . .?"
- "What surprised you the most when . . .?"
- "What would you do different the next time around?"

And be interested, enthusiastic, and complimentary with your responses: "How exhilarating." "How courageous." "How insightful." One rule: mean it! One of my daughter's favorite expressions when I tell her about a joyful experience is, "What fun!" Her enthusiastic response always makes me feel good.

Get to Where You Want to Be After small talk, go from light conversation to business talk any time you can make a natural transition. If you're looking for it, you'll find an opening. In just a few words, you want to arouse the person's curiosity and make arrangements to meet again, such as in the following instances.

You meet an old school buddy outside the grocery store. After the usual small talk, she asks what you've been up to. How beautiful is that? You could answer with something like, "Glad you asked. I can't believe my good fortune. I'm really enthused about . . ." You're off and running. Continue with something along these lines: "It's fun, easy, and profitable. I'd love to give you the details. It would be a wonderful match for your warm personality. Let's meet over a cup of coffee, catch up, and I'll fill you in." That's how I would say it. You, of course, would choose words that work for you. Let's try a tougher one.

You're at a social gathering. You seek out a humorous and outgoing work associate of the host. After the small talk, what do you say? Something like, "I'm so glad we had a chance to talk. I noticed people gravitated to you. Now I know why. You're fun to be around." or "You have a wild sense of humor." (When you give the *why* of the compliment, it rings true.) Continue with something along these lines: "You'd be a perfect fit in my business. Let's meet for lunch or coffee. I'd love to give you some thought-provoking details."

I did a short, informal survey with people from different backgrounds: a homemaker, a business leader, a salesperson, and an engineer. I asked them to tell me what would make them receptive to giving a stranger their telephone number. These were their answers:

- "If they intrigued me"
- "If they kept it light"
- "If they seemed *genuinely* enthused and convinced"
- "If they were low-key"

- "If I sensed I could trust them"
- "If they seemed self-assured"
- "If they knew someone I knew"

I asked myself what characteristics attracted me most to those I didn't know. The first descriptions that popped into my head were warm and friendly, interesting, and confident.

It's your turn. Have you ever been drawn to a stranger, but never thought about why? (Good looks don't count!) Think about it now. What was it about them that made you want to get to know them? Jot it down in your binder.

You should also make it a habit to keep track of all business leads. If you're the type who writes important information on envelopes, receipts, or grocery lists, and then you find yourself saying, "I know her name and number are here *somewhere*," fight your usual habits. Throw out all of those scraps of paper and create an organized system for leads.

Set up a database that contains names, addresses, where you met, and what was said. File alphabetically and by date of next contact. Salespeople have used a card system for years, and it still works. There are also computer programs that simplify this step. Ask a leader who swears by it, and see if the initial investment of time and cost works for you. Sometimes it takes "keeping in touch" till the time is right. That person you least expected to give you a yes could end up being your best customer or your next team superstar.

Using the Phone to Open the Door

When it comes to new business, how you handle it depends on the purpose of the call. When the purpose is to gain a new team member, the ideal use of the phone is to set an appointment, not to close a sale. Whenever possible, you want the advantages of a person-to-person meeting, which is a chance to establish a relationship, make note of the environment, and read body language. Plus, the prospect doesn't have the advantage of seeing your smiling face, picking up on your open body language, or feeling the energy and confidence generated by your firm handshake over the phone. But sometimes the ideal simply isn't feasible. When you need to do business over the phone, remember that your voice must carry the entire message. And if you're feeling down, or lacking in confidence, your prospect will sense it. The following tips will help you be your most effective.

Get Ready I remember Earl Nightingale pointing out that, "Actions trigger feelings just as feelings trigger actions." Since you want to feel confident and sound energetic and friendly, here are some suggested actions that can help you do just that:

- Dress for business. Sure it's great being comfy in pajamas. After all, isn't comfort one of the advantages of a home-based business? *Yes*, if you're at the computer or doing paperwork. *No*, if you're on the phone with a prospect. Any dress that could detract from your feeling and sounding professional is not worth that cozy feeling.

- Use the old mirror trick. Put a large mirror right where you'll be able to get a good look at your face as you're talking. You'll start smiling right away. Actually, it's tough not to laugh when you first get a glimpse of yourself, and that's good too. Make faces or give yourself a little pep talk—anything that puts you in a positive frame of mind *before* you pick up the phone.

- Make brief notes. What's your objective on this call? What key words will get you there? Jot them down.

- Psych yourself up. Assume positive results. Remind yourself that you're *not* begging for a favor, you're offering an opportunity.

- Make sure you blocked out this time for business; no barking dogs, no screaming children, no rumbling washing machine, and no family member who just *must* talk to you.

Now you're ready!

Make an Immediate Connection It takes just seconds for the person on the other end to decide if they will give you some of their precious time or not. Your first few words must not only convey warmth, confidence, and energy, but must also give the prospect a reason to stay with you.

Naming a mutual friend or business associate or reminding them of where and how you met is okay for starters, but it won't buy you a whole lotta time.

Arouse Their Curiosity Give a sincere compliment, cover a benefit to them, tap your humor, say something surprising—or all four!

The following are some phone-starter ideas:

- "I was the three-foot-tall lady devouring the shrimp." (A description of me. Well, almost—I'm four feet eleven.)
- "You're so outgoing and spontaneous. I kept thinking about our conversation and knew I had to give you a call. I know you'd be great at . . ."
- "This may seem to come at you from out of the blue, but I want to tell you about this exciting, lucrative business that would be perfect for a self-starter like you."
- "You owe it to yourself to find out why this is such an exciting opportunity. There are absolutely no strings attached."
- "More and more corporate women are starting their own businesses because it's flexible and profitable."

If the objective is to book a presentation, your approach would be a little different and you can go for a decision over the phone:

- "I didn't get a chance to speak with you last night, but knowing you're such a fan of (the product/service), I wanted to make sure to let you know the benefits of hosting a presentation this month."
- "I just learned of an exciting new product we'll be introducing next week, and you were the first person I thought of. I'd love to get your reaction to it."

Use any current statistics, trends, or news to your advantage. Is the growth rate of your company impressive? Is your product or service on the cutting edge? Can you think of an attention grabber in the news that's relevant to what you sell? Do you have a new product, a new program, an exciting promotion that gives you a reason to contact prospects?

Get to the Meat of the Call At this point in the conversation you either set an appointment or cover the benefits of your proposal: "I'd love to get together with you, bum a cup of coffee, and cover the specifics."

Ask if it's an okay time to talk for a few minutes. If the prospect is running out the door, there's no way they will be receptive to what you have to say, no matter how enticing it sounds.

Give a few choices for when you can call back if you learn you called at an inopportune time. *Don't* leave it up to the prospect to set a callback time. (Start by giving a window of time on the same day.)

Say you'll be in the neighborhood only if it's the truth. (There's no bigger turnoff than an overused line.) Then, give specifics: "I'm meeting Sarah Murphy at 127 Elm, the next street over from you, at 10:00 AM. I can drop by at 11:00."

Stress that she's not obligated to make a decision if you sense hesitancy. I've often said, "I'll just give you the specifics so you can decide whether this is right for you or not."

And when it fits, I've said something more personal, like, "And besides, we clicked so well, it's great to have an excuse to see you again," or, "It gives me an excuse to see that garden you were bragging about."

Stick to a Planned Format If your goal is to get a decision, send written information in advance so you can refer to it during the call. Include a friendly note saying you'll be calling soon.

Keep your call short and to the point. Unless it is absolutely necessary, don't get trapped into long explanations over the phone. Have a reason to follow up: "I'll get detailed information in the mail today. I'll answer any questions when we meet Tuesday. Let's set a time that works for you so I can cover more details."

Remember: Be real. Be warm. Be conversational. Use words you would use over the kitchen table.

Follow up immediately so you reinforce the information while it's fresh in her mind. If possible, send a text message or e-mail immediately. Then send a warm, friendly note reviewing all details.

What do you say if you get the dreaded voice mail? First, *expect* to get it so you know what you'll say when you do. I've heard some pathetic, meandering messages when the caller was thrown off by an automated message. Your goal is to be brief, sound confident, and arouse curiosity. Sound familiar? Here are some thought starters:

- "Hi _____, I met you at _____'s and wanted to fill you in on an interesting opportunity that may just be perfect for you. I'll call back again or you can reach me at (number) between _____ and _____."

- "Hi _____, I loved our stimulating discussion and have something exciting to share that I didn't bring up at the time. I'll call again, or you can reach me at (number)."

By making your phone personality as engaging as your actual personality, you can greatly increase the number of calls that result in appointments, new recruits, and yeses.

Do the Math

I'd be letting you down if I didn't point out that no matter how quick you are on your feet, no matter how much you hone your sales skills, you won't see impressive results unless you know what it takes to get the results you want.

If you've been in sales more than two weeks you have probably heard something like, "It's a numbers game." Although that's not my favorite expression, it's true. Yes, determination, skill, confidence, all that good stuff, plays a huge role in your success. But if you aren't consistently setting aside time to find leads, if you aren't seeing and talking to enough people, no amount of ability will get you where you want to go. You've read it before, but it bears repeating: skill + contacts = success.

If you're wondering how many contacts are enough, first figure out the results you want. Then determine your current percentage of positive outcomes based on the number of contacts you make, say over a six-week period. Those figures will give you the number you're looking for. Of course, if your percentage rate of success is *really* low (ouch!), you need to determine why.

Lets say you notice you average one new team member for every five calls. If your goal for the month is four new members, plan to have a minimum of twenty interviews. It's a good idea to know those percentages in every category of your business, so keep a record. It doesn't have to be anything fancy; hash marks will do.

You can only measure improvement by knowing where you started! And this journey we're taking together *will* increase your percentages. *Believe* it.

Ten Little Gems

1. Only give a compliment you truly mean. Others can tell the difference between real and phony.

2. Convey confidence and enthusiasm in your words and tone. This is a must. (I seem to be singing a familiar tune.) If necessary, practice privately with a tape recorder.

3. Remind yourself of the value of what you're offering. You wouldn't have chosen your product or service if you didn't think it was beneficial to others, now would you?

4. Choose words that fit your personality and your style: realness, realness, REALNESS.

5. Look for early signs of whether you're talking to a Tess, Bill, or Dora. (Remember, they're the three personality types: Touchy-feely, Bottom Line, and Details, Details.)

6. Choose adjectives that will create interest in your product or service, words like the following: *exciting, lucrative, groundbreaking, fascinating, innovative, challenging,* and *fun.* You get the idea.

7. Take risks. It takes courage, but remember that pushing yourself out of your comfort zone is a good thing.

8. Ask yourself, "What's the worst thing that can happen? What's the best thing that can happen?" Remember, if you get a no, it's not the end of the world. Repeat after me: "It's not the end of the world."

9. Remember my favorite adage, one I've told myself whenever I've had the queasy feeling that comes from the fear that I'll get a negative response: You'll never know unless you ask! (In *my* case I'd probably still be single.)

10. Reach out and connect frequently. The more you do, the easier it gets and the better you get at it. And when you get better at it, you also get more business. What an exciting circle of events!

When I was a distributor, I wrote a weekly newsletter. I ended each one with the same four words. After all these years, I feel compelled to say them again. Are they corny? Perhaps. Are they heartfelt? *Absolutely.*

Go get 'em, tigers!

QUICK RECAP

- *Make* opportunities to meet new people.
- Learn how to approach others in various social and business situations.
- Know how to move from small talk to business talk.
- Have an organized way to keep track of and follow up on leads.
- Use the phone to open the door to future business.
- Remember that the more people you see and talk to, the greater your chances of ongoing success.

BINDER TIME

- Thinking of what you have done up till now, identify two areas where you need to get better at continuing to build your business.
- Make a list of actions you can take to improve in those areas. For instance, if you've had difficulty getting results over the phone in the past, list two reasons you think your phone skills don't seem to be working. What can you do to overcome those challenges? Write down a few sentences you could use as attention getters, or what you'll say if you get the dreaded voice mail.
- Once you've written your list, decide what small action you can take for each weak area within the next five days.

CHAPTER 10

Adding to the Flock

Whether you're a part-timer or a career salesperson, recruiting can make a considerable difference in how much money you make. That alone is reason to get good at it. And if you plan to lead a team, it will be the lifeblood of your organization: no new people equals not much future growth, and perhaps not much future. So what does it take to be a strong recruiter? First, let's get the obvious out of the way. You know how to cover the key questions: (1) How much do I make? (2) How difficult is it, both to do and to get business? and (3) How much will it cost me to get started? You also know to stress the desirability of your product or service, the fine reputation of your company, and the support readily available to new people.

Your company brochure likely lays these benefits out in a logical order. Become thoroughly comfortable using it. If needed, add a few personal notes to the brochure to keep you on track. You might also want to practice aloud with a friend to get your presentation down pat.

The purpose of this chapter is not to rehash what you know, but to give you ideas that will increase your percentage of yeses. Speaking of percentages, here's something you should consider. If you interview two people in a month and recruit one, that's a 50 percent average. It sounds impressive, but we both know it's not so hot. If you have ten interviews in a month and get five yeses, now you're talkin'! Without belaboring the point, no amount of expertise will help much unless you hold a consistent number of interviews. The formula, one more time: skill + contacts = success.

Okay, now let's cover how to get the best results from those efforts.

Upping Your Percentages

These suggestions can make an enormous difference in the outcome of your interviews. Knowing the key points to cover is the beginning, but knowing the subtle things that result in more yeses will make you a pro.

Check Out Your Assumptions Before you open your car door, assume the result of the interview will be a yes. Have the mind-set that you're interviewing *them*—they're not interviewing *you*.

Make a Connection Your goal is to go from salesperson to new acquaintance in a short time. You do that by taking a few minutes for small talk. There are no pat words for small talk. Sometimes an icebreaker just comes to you and sometimes you have information that's perfect for relaxing you both. Think a bit ahead. Ask yourself, "Did something happen lately or on the way that was interesting, funny, or frustrating? Is there anything I have in common with this person: a shared interest or background, a mutual friend, young children or college kids, a hobby? Did I read or hear something recently that's relevant and that would be of interest to this prospect?"

Although fewer interviews are now held in the home, when they are, there's much to notice and comment on, such as the garden, the artwork, the décor, and the children. I once noticed a really frightening gargoyle on a prospect's porch. It gave me a great opening and led to an interesting conversation.

The one absolute—aside from being warm, friendly, and complimentary—is to be real. (Nothing is a faster turn-off than overdone praise or gushing. Ugh!)

No Cookie-cutter Interviews Even though you follow a pat formula, every interview should be personalized based on what you know about the prospect. Why? Because when you match your prospect's needs and goals with your offer, you're more likely to get to yes. For example, if you know that young children are an issue, you would obviously stress the "beauty of flexibility" and the ability to be there during crucial times in children's lives. If you know a new home is in your prospect's future, you would certainly stress how the additional income would make it possible sooner.

Knowledge Is Power The more you know going in, the better. Do you know why she agreed to meet with you? If not, ask her up front. Does she have a family? If so, do you know the age range of her children? What's her work experience and how would that experience be an advantage in sales? What other life experiences would give you additional information that would help you match her background with your offer? What stands out about her personality that would be an asset in business? (It can be something you picked up on immediately, what you were told, or what you noted if you met previously.)

You can learn much more by simply observing and asking a few questions. When it's a natural transition early in the conversation, say something like, "So I can show you how this business could be a perfect match for your needs and interests, may I ask a few questions that will help me get to know you a little better?" Here are some examples of questions you might ask.

- "What gives you the most personal satisfaction?"
- "What would you say is just one of your strengths?"
- "What motivates you to try something new?"
- "What accomplishment are you most proud of?"
- "What would you like next that money could buy?"

As you read the questions, which one or two would you be most comfortable asking? Can you think of one other? Imagine the many ways you could tie in *any* of her answers to your proposition.

Say you asked her to tell you just one of her strengths, and she answered, "I guess the first thing I thought of was my sense of humor. People tell me I'm funny." You'd be off and running. How is the wonderful ability to make people laugh an asset in sales? *Now* you're talking her language!

Tell It Like It Is What you say should match up with what she will experience. I can't emphasize this enough: *Don't let your zeal to recruit get in the way of your honesty.* It will come back to bite you.

That means that when you talk about profit, be sure to also allow for normal expenses. If you give examples of those who make six-figure incomes, point out that they are the top performers who treat their business as a full-time career.

Clarify that whether she chooses a part-time or full-time opportunity, she should plan to set aside a specific number of hours each week for her business. Ask what will work for her. If she's thinking part-time is five hours a week, tactfully let her know that won't cut it. Suggest the reasonable amount of time she should invest to get the results she wants. The beauty of being straightforward initially is that *she* understands that she needs to make a certain effort, even as a part-timer, and *you* have established expectations that you can review when encouraging and coaching her. Remember, you won't detract from an opportunity by being honest and spelling out expectations—you'll *add* to it.

The Interview Is Not a Monologue There are two pitfalls you should be careful to avoid when interviewing: (1) becoming so enamored with what you're saying that you don't want to stop talking, and (2) being so apprehensive about hearing a negative that you just keep rolling along. Pause now and then to allow your prospect to respond. Ask periodic questions to check her reaction. Here are some examples.

- "How does it sound so far?"
- "Does that make sense?"
- "Have I explained that clearly?"
- "Any questions so far?"
- "Does that answer your concern?"
- "Does that work with your schedule?"

The incredible benefit of asking these kinds of questions throughout the interview is that they give you enormous insight into whether she understands and how much (or how little) you have captured her interest.

Use Pauses Effectively Pause after making a key point or when shifting from one subject to another. Pause when asked a question so that you have time to choose your words.

Know How You're Coming Across Do you sound confident? Assured? Warm? Friendly? Do you keep eye contact? Smile? All this will relax your prospect and help her warm to your words.

Watch for Verbal and Nonverbal Clues If you sense confusion or you're getting a negative or disinterested reaction, address it on the spot. I've seen a prospect's eyes glaze over as she valiantly tried to absorb all the levels of a complex compensation plan when the first few levels would have been enough for her to hear about initially.

I've also seen a prospect sold and unsold during the same interview. I shudder when I hear an obvious buying signal like, "It sounds really good," and then hear the salesperson go on and on and on instead of closing and getting a signed application right then.

I've seen a prospect whose closed, rigid body language and negative stare went unnoticed by an exuberant interviewer. That was the time to address how the prospect was responding by saying something like, "I'm sensing you have some concern. Would you please tell me what you're thinking?"

Don't be afraid to be real and honest—you'll get realness and honesty back. Then you can respond to what she's *really* thinking. Plus, you'll be respected for your openness.

Finally, just as in handling objections in *any* selling situation, *don't let an objection spook you*. It simply tells you that the prospect is interested but has a concern. And you'll want to *know* that concern, because unless you answer it satisfactorily, you'll find it tough to close. (For example, if the prospect says, "I can't see myself in sales," she needs to know why she would be good at it.) Hear it, acknowledge it, answer it, and move on.

When You Get a Yes

Take the next three steps, pronto! Why the urgency? Because once enthusiastic, warm, optimistic you walks out, fear, regret, and insecurity walk in.

First, make sure you line up an action the new person can take immediately. Why? Once someone takes an action, it cements his or her decision. (Think about the nervous, unsure bachelor. When he starts looking at rings, he's on his way to hearing the wedding march.)

Quick, list three things the new person can do that day that will keep her excited about her decision. Jot them down in your binder.

Second, send a note, preferably from the car, welcoming her, telling her how happy you are to have her on your team, and reminding her that she made a wise decision. When possible, follow up immediately with a text message or e-mail. You might even want to get creative. Humor often works. One leader I know of mails a pair of socks with a note that reads, "Use these if you get cold feet."

Third, check back the next day to see how she's doing and answer any questions she may have. She needs to hear from enthusiastic, friendly, optimistic you—and soon!

Don't Close the Book on the Noes

Circumstances change, attitudes change, and needs change. A no today could be a yes down the road. Keep a dated list, along with memory-jogging notes. Check back after a month or two.

I learned this the hard way. I interviewed a charming lady who gave me what sounded like an absolute no. Six months later she walked into a sales meeting with another leader. Her situation had changed. What was even tougher for me to swallow was that she went on to be a top performer and, eventually, a top leader.

An initial no may not be a permanent no. Some people are slower at making decisions and may just need time to think it through. When you call a few months later you may find a receptive person on the other end of the line. In fact, I'd bet that if you asked twenty people whether they said yes to an opportunity the first time they were asked, you'd get a hefty number of noes.

Ending on a touchy-feely note, I can't think of a much more satisfying or joyful experience than seeing someone grow personally and professionally and knowing *you* were the one who opened that door for them.

QUICK RECAP

- To see measurable growth, hold a consistent number of interviews.
- Assume from the start that you will get a yes.
- Practice the art of small talk so you quickly go from salesperson to new acquaintance.
- Learn as much as possible about the prospect before and during the interview so you can personalize it based on each prospect's needs and interests.
- See the interview as give-and-take. Involve the prospect.
- Recognize buying signals so you know when and how to close.
- Always tell it like it is.
- Just as with your presentation, getting more yeses is the ultimate goal. So you also want to be a pro at overcoming objections and closing. If you're shaky in either, check out chapter five before you even think of doing that next interview.

BINDER TIME

- Write down what you think is easiest about the interview. Why do you think that is?
- As you read this chapter, a few suggestions should have "hit you over the head." List two things you want to do or change immediately. When will you do this? Once you have made these changes, come back to this section and fill in your insights. (*Yes,* it's worth the time.)

CHAPTER 11

The Fine Art of Leadership

*How sad to know that some succeed not because
of their leaders—but in spite of them.*

If there's *any* subject that's been written about, discussed, dissected, and examined in detail ad infinitum, it's leadership, and for good reason. Effective leaders can bring about enormous positive change, whether we're talking about parenting or politics, science or sociology, or leading a sales team.

And just as top salespeople don't fit a neat mold, the same is certainly true of top sales leaders. They come in all sizes and shapes, have widely different backgrounds, and have dramatically different personalities. However, the most respected in the field have qualities in common that set them apart.

They Have Integrity They keep their word. They're ethical—whether dealing with their company, their customers, or their team. They can be trusted with confidential information. They don't gossip. If something doesn't square with their values, they have the courage to speak up.

They Don't Play Favorites They consider options and weigh decisions, taking into account all involved. If there's a problem between the team and the company, they represent the team's interests as well as the company's interests.

They Care About Their Teams They recognize and respect each person's individuality and strengths. They want team members to succeed for themselves, not just for their own personal gain.

They're Confident They're aware of their ability, yet even though they're sure of themselves, they don't pretend to know it all or be it all. They don't feel they need to prove anything.

They're Competent They know what they're talking about and prove it by setting a consistently good example.

As you read through the list, if you identified one or two qualities that aren't, as yet, your strengths, don't go getting down on yourself. The list is simply a reminder of what to shoot for. We *all* learn bit by bit to get better and better at what we do.

I was just as green and insecure when I became a leader as when I held my first presentation. I recall driving home with my first manager company car and saying to my husband, "Enjoy the car, because I have no idea how long I'll be able keep it." I wasn't exactly brimming with confidence. I realized later that those feelings weren't unique to me. I had a lot to learn, but that didn't mean I couldn't make it.

As new leaders, that initial adrenaline rush, the thrill of the accomplishment, and the close-knit relationship we have with our teams are all we need to get us off the ground: It's in the *doing* that we learn. The next chapters are guaranteed to make that learning quicker and easier. Trust me.

Look Behind You—They're Following

Being a sales leader is considerably different than being an independent salesperson. When you were on your own, you were in complete control. Your success came from *your* efforts alone. Now that you have a team, you're one step removed from that control. Most of your results will come from the efforts of others.

And unlike an employer–employee relationship, which requires compliance, your team follows not because they *have* to but because they *want* to. They give you their loyalty voluntarily. So what does it take to earn that loyalty? How do you become the kind of leader who makes your team want to be successful as much for you as for themselves?

Get to Know Your Team

If you asked me, I could come pretty close to describing what it takes to build a successful team in a few simple sentences: Love them. Recognize their strengths. Appreciate them. Push them beyond what they think possible. Guide them little by little. Praise them every step of the way.

Although yours is a business relationship, it's vital that you know your team far beyond their names on a printout. When you take the time to learn about their backgrounds and family situations, their uniqueness and their dreams, two positives are bound to happen: They will feel special, and you will learn how best to help them.

Here's a quick test. Do you know the following about the members of your immediate team?

- their birthdays
- the names of their immediate family
- the ages of their children
- what they're most proud of
- their strengths
- what motivates them most

How did you do? If the answer is "Pretty good," congrats! If the answer is "Not so hot," you'll want to work on it because this information is critical.

Let's take a closer look at how those six bits of information can play out. Notice how the first four elements help build relationships and the last two help form winners.

Birthdays Sending a card and brief note says they're more than just numbers on a page. Acknowledging other life passages—such as a graduation, a marriage, a new grandchild, or the death of a loved one—says even more.

Family Calling their children, their spouse, or their ailing mother by name lets them know you care about them as people.

Kids Knowing the ages of their children gives you a much clearer understanding of how they must divide their time between work and home.

Pride Learning what they're most proud of gives you insight into what matters most to them, their *values*. That knowledge helps you see things from their perspective and allows you to speak to that.

People Grow Through Relationships

When there's a relationship that goes *beyond* just the business (I'm not talking personal, gossipy stuff), when the followers truly believe that the leader has their personal interests at heart, respects them, and cares for them, great things can happen. I know, I've been to countless sales conferences and interviewed the biggies, those getting top recognition. Many were motivated to be on stage almost as much for their leaders as for themselves. The affection and gratitude they expressed never ceased to amaze me. It was obvious that they knew their leaders not only helped them, but also that they truly cared about them.

Strengths Identifying and utilizing team members' individual strengths helps everybody win. The individual gains the confidence needed to succeed in business, and you and your team gain the benefit of her talents.

A detail-oriented born organizer would love to help you pull together a complex event—it's a win-win situation, hands down!

Someone who has been in a helping profession, such as nursing or teaching, can be an asset when instructing others.

Someone who is a nurturing parent may be great at spoiling customers *and* encouraging the team.

Someone who has been a leader may relish taking on more of a leadership role early on. She may also want to go further faster. Be ready to match her energy with your effort.

Speaking of utilizing team members' strengths, here's one for the books. A savvy leader once had a team member who always seemed to find something to complain about. At meetings, she inevitably saw the glass as half empty. She was often in the spotlight, but for the wrong reasons. When her leader (a wise lady) discovered that the complainer was a talented amateur photographer, she asked her to be the official team photographer. The negative comments practically disappeared. She was still in the spotlight, but for the right reasons. Everybody smiled, and not just for the camera.

Motivation Make it a rule to know what the individuals on your team are working for, their personal motivations, because that's what will keep them going long after that initial enthusiasm wears off. *When you know what team members want or need most,* you can help them stay focused by painting a mental picture of how it will feel when they get it. Many times someone's motivation is obvious, but sometimes it's not.

A good example of this is a manager I worked with, Yvonne, a quiet, sophisticated college grad. She didn't speak often, but when she did, her words carried weight with the team. I thought Yvonne was motivated strictly by the money she could make. I was only half right.

When I asked all my managers what motivated them most, these were Yvonne's exact words, "I would kill to walk across the stage."

She loved the recognition, and I hadn't a clue. From then on, when I encouraged Yvonne to make a goal, you can bet I painted a picture of the "glory" part—along with the dollars part.

Rarely are we humans motivated by just one thing. We want material things *and* we have emotional needs. You could want to be debt free, vacation in Tuscany, or pay for a child's tuition, and also be turned on by the idea of helping others, getting recognition, taking on a challenge, or proving something to your mother-in-law. Sure, personal motivation is complex, yet to the attuned leader it can be obvious.

If you're a leader of women, you have many areas to focus on. Today's woman is far different from yesterday's woman. Years ago, we were told that the husband provided the cake and the wife provided the icing—and that was often true. Today's woman could be providing the whole meal and cooking it to boot! Today's woman is driven to succeed for numerous and varied reasons. She may be a struggling single parent who needs to support her family. She may be working toward an advanced degree. She may be a former corporate leader who wants autonomy and flexibility; or an "empty nester" looking for an exciting pastime, others to nurture, or a new identity. Get to know your team members and what they want the most out of the business.

Although I have spoken predominantly of working with woman, *much* has changed in a man's world too. We *do* see husbands as full-time caregivers. We *do* know that the man's role has changed considerably over the years. Many men now take on chores at home that match a woman's efforts. And having another identity and challenge, along with the financial rewards and recognition that follows in direct sales, can be equally appealing to men. If it's a resource you haven't pursued, seriously consider it.

When you have a clear understanding of what team members are working for, you can *expect* them to work hard without fearing you will turn them off. When others understand that you're pushing them so they can get what they dearly want or need, it's tough, if not impossible, for them to resent you for it! And when they get it, they'll be grateful for your every nudge along the way.

Thinking of your immediate team, can you make an educated guess as to what motivates each member? (Remember, it can be more than one thing.) If you're stymied, do what I did and ask each one. Or you might have them write it down. When you get it, don't let that priceless information go to waste. Use it when appropriate, to encourage them, to help them bounce back, and to push them to grow.

> Food for thought: Unless they know you care, it's difficult for them to give you their loyalty. Unless you know who they are, it's difficult for you to influence what they do.

The Power of Sincere Praise

I'm constantly blown away when I see the effect sincere praise can have on another. It can light up a face, boost spirits, and let someone know they're respected and appreciated, and it warms the heart of both the giver and the receiver. But more than that, sincere praise is often what helps others gain the confidence needed to grow. The following is just one of many examples.

She came to meetings, sat in the back, and kept to herself. She was indistinguishable in dress and manner. For some reason I can't remember now, I made an effort to get to know her better. Besides selling, I learned that she ran a small farm, practically single-handedly. For starters, she canned, baked, milked cows, and handled the birthing of calves. I began to believe there was hardly anything she *couldn't* do. She was tough and gentle at the same time. I was incredibly impressed with her work ethic and in awe of her many talents, and I told her so. I appreciated and respected her enormously, and she knew it.

Before long she began to sit up front. She became a little more talkative. She made eye contact more often. And her sales increased. Was my praise and admiration the sole reason for the change? Perhaps not, but I'm convinced it was a key factor.

Know how to give praise. Besides being sincere, be specific. When you make general statements like, "You're great!" "Good job!" or "Nice going!" you risk sounding phony or manipulative. Avoid that pitfall by spelling out exactly what it is that deserves the praise. For example, you might let the team member know the following:

- What actual dollar figure increase in sales she had this month over last month
- What percentage of yeses versus calls made was impressive
- What personal quality of hers made the meeting run smoothly
- Why others listen when she speaks
- What quality you respect and admire about her

Make a concerted effort to lavish praise on new team members: New people feel insecure no matter *what* they've accomplished in the past. They're on unfamiliar ground. Sincere praise is music to their ears. From the start, look for their strengths and qualities and hold those up to a mirror so they can see them, too. Here are some examples of what you might say.

- "You're so warm and outgoing. I've noticed that people like you immediately."
- "I'm in awe of your organizational skills. I could sure learn from you."
- "Your past accomplishments are a big asset. People will look to you for answers because you know from experience."
- "You love these products, and it shows. Your enthusiasm rubs off on everybody."

- "You're so funny. People are obviously drawn to you because they love being around you."

Early recognition builds confidence when it's needed most.

Recognize a *stretch*. An experienced team member with a good performance record wouldn't expect you to recognize her routine efforts. (And if you *did*, she might question your sincerity.) But an insecure, inexperienced person who makes five calls in a row has stepped *way* out of her comfort zone. She needs and deserves your praise.

Avoid cookie-cutter recognition. If team members hear you saying the same thing to others, it loses its value, big time! Choose your words carefully so they fit both the accomplishment and the receiver.

Remember too, knowing how to give recognition doesn't stop with business. You may be surprised at how family and friends respond to honest, specific praise. So pass it on. Your life will be richer for it.

Share Your Energy and Optimism

It's hard to define these two qualities, but you certainly know them when you see them—or perhaps it's when you *feel* them. When I was a distributor for a large direct sales company, we were back ordered, big time, on an incredibly popular gift that hosts received when they had specific sales and future presentations booked.

I was frustrated by the long delay and having to mollify upset salespeople daily. I called headquarters and spoke with the VP of Sales. When I hung up the phone, my husband asked if I had any good news. I said, "No, but I sure feel better." We both laughed. It wasn't what the VP said. (He explained the reason for the delay, and he was empathetic, but I wasn't getting even one carton sooner.) Then why did I feel better? It was because of the *way* he said it.

Think of someone who lifts you up whenever you talk with them. What is it about that person that makes you feel that way? Is it their warm tone, their energy level, the joy in their voice, their eye contact, your sense that they really care what you say? *That's* what your people need from you.

Suppose It's a Bad Day

We all have good days and bad days. (I remember that same VP saying that the only person with a smile on his face every morning is someone with a hanger in his mouth.) If you aren't feeling energized and optimistic *before* you connect with any team member, give yourself a pep talk, take a walk, do whatever it takes to get yourself "up." Remember, they're watching and listening.

Have High Expectations

At the beginning of each leadership seminar I asked the group to think of a leader—such as a parent, teacher, or boss—who had a considerable positive influence in their lives, someone they respected highly. Then I asked them to list the qualities or characteristics that prompted them to think of that person.

Although I've done this exercise with hundreds of participants, almost to the person they have listed "high expectations" as a key characteristic of the leader they chose. They often went on to say that if it weren't for the leader's expectations, they likely would not have been as successful—or even successful at all!

The same is true of those who look to you for guidance. You can be kind, empathetic, and caring, and at the same time have high expectations. They aren't mutually exclusive. Your role is to help your team stretch and grow, and it starts by expecting things of them.

> Don't let the fear that you will lose them
> rob you of the power to lead them.

You may be thinking that it sounds good, but wondering what you can reasonably expect of your team. For starters, you can expect them to

- Keep their word. If they say they will make X number of calls, they should. If they say they will attend a meeting, they should. If they say they will meet you for a coaching session, they should.
- Set aside some time for their business on a regular basis. Plant that seed early on. In the interview or shortly after, ask them how much time they plan to devote to their business weekly.
- Take advantage of the training available to them.
- Have integrity and follow company guidelines.
- Keep up with company promotions, new products, etc.
- Match your efforts.

If they don't meet your expectations, how you handle it depends on the individual situation. If it were an ethical issue, for example, you would confront them immediately and reach an agreement about what has to change. If you were convinced, through their actions, that they weren't making a sincere effort to get business, you might adjust your support accordingly. And sometimes, based on the circumstances, you may decide that they just need a little nudge, reminder, or encouragement.

Know Their Style

I remember them well. They both had spirit and spunk; they both were giving, caring people; they both were hard workers; and they both were successful managers on my team. Yet they had dramatically different personalities. One was soft-spoken and sensitive, the consummate lady. The other was outspoken, brash, and fun loving. (She drove stock cars for kicks.)

My communication style changed considerably when coaching each. If I didn't choose my words carefully, the sensitive lady might cry. Meanwhile, I could tell the stock car racer she needed to get off her buns and make more of an effort, and we'd both laugh. The point? Make note of your team members' unique differences and speak to them in their language.

Help Them Think on Their Own

Although I don't know you personally, I *do* know two things about you: you're a problem solver and you're in a hurry. I know that because you're a sales leader, and when a team member is struggling with a business problem, your natural tendency is to want to fix it quickly and move on. (Of course, that's true of parents, too.)

But when you jump in and try to take care of a situation you don't help followers think on their own. That doesn't mean you can't give advice and guidance. It does mean that you shouldn't immediately come up with a solution or, like a mom when her child gets a boo-boo, instantly try to make it all better.

Tough as it is, first make sure you understand by actively listening, and then ask open-ended questions like the following:

- "What do you think is causing that?"
- "What seems like the best solution?"
- "What do you think needs to change?"

You may be amazed at how often they come up with the perfect answer. If they're still struggling, *then* step in and guide them to a solution.

Many times, after others have sought me out for advice, they'll say something like "I'm so glad we talked," or "You helped me so much." I smile inside, because I know perfectly well that all I did was paraphrase what they said; they knew what to do all along!

The Fine Art of Coaching

I shy away from sounding dogmatic, but I'll go out on a limb on this one and say that coaching is the most critical and rewarding part of being an effective leader. When you can help a team member understand what's getting in the way of her success, guide her to make changes, and see her grow, that's big-time power *and* big-time satisfaction.

You coach informally every time you help others discover what they need to do or change to reach their goals. It's a good idea to meet with team members in person periodically, especially those you believe aren't really trying, or who *are* trying but aren't getting results. No matter where, when, or with whom your coaching takes place, it will be far more effective when you use the following seven steps:

1. **Go in prepared.** Know the figures. What's not working? Is it that her activity is sporadic, that her sales are below the average for the area, or that she's not sponsoring? Perhaps she's had zero activity for some time. You both know there's a problem, so state the specifics.

2. **Remind her of her goals.** Here's why knowing what they're working for is so valuable. Say something as simple as, "I know you want to help Sam get a college education, and I want you to have the satisfaction of seeing it happen. So let's work on it together."

3. **Determine the reason.** You're not likely to have a clear idea of what's causing the problem. You could make an educated guess, but only the person who has the problem really knows. So ask open-ended questions like these:

- "Knowing how much you want to keep growing, why do you think you hit this roadblock?"
- "Since you've been devoting considerable time to your business, why do you think you're not getting the results you deserve?"
- "You were so enthused and optimistic initially. What do you think changed?"

Be aware that often the first thing she says may not be the real reason but the one that sounds good. She may blame her hectic schedule when the real reason is that she's afraid to pick up the phone. She may say she hasn't a clue why she's not getting yeses when the real reason is that she's shaky on the close. She may say she's decided that selling just isn't for her when the real reason is that she's heard so many noes that she's discouraged.

Here's where your ability to actively listen is so valuable. If you keep clarifying what you understand her to be saying, she's likely to get to the root of the problem all by herself.

4. **Brainstorm solutions.** Determining what to do should be a joint decision, because unless she's involved, nothing will likely change. It's a problem-solving session between two people who both have the same goal—to turn things around.

5. **Decide who will do what when.** What can you do to help? What's her end of the bargain? Be specific regarding actions, dates, and times. When you challenge her to do something, give her a reachable goal. For example, if you ask her to book a certain number of presentations and she makes the effort and fails, she will feel bad no matter what you say. When you ask her to make a certain number of calls a day for three days, it's completely within her power. Once she's done it, she's succeeded and she will feel good.

6. **Build in accountability.** This is key, because without it, your agreement loses power. Set a date and time to check back to see what's happened. Has there been a change for the better? Can you help in another way?

7. **Praise any effort.** If she observed a top performer in action, before asking what she learned, congratulate her for wanting to learn. If she makes ten calls each day for two or three days, no matter what the outcome, praise her effort. You can work together on improving her results.

When people are given direction and are made accountable, they often surprise even themselves.

When Enough Is Enough

I was driving down the street a while back and noticed a message on a huge sign in front of an office building. I started laughing so hard I nearly drove up on the sidewalk. The sign read, "If the horse is dead, it is prudent to dismount."

Good advice when you're struggling with the question of just how long to hang in there with someone you have coached repeatedly. If she's not matching your efforts even though you have given her several chances, you may be guilty of what I call the "missionary attitude." You want to save them all.

That's admirable but not logical, because you can't save them all. (It sure eats up a ton of time when you try!) Borrowing from baseball, it's probably time to use the old "three strikes and you're out" logic. When a team member has not kept her promises three times in a short period of time and has no logical explanations, you have a pretty good clue that she's not trying. Unless her attitude changes, let her do her own thing and move on to those who deserve your faith and support.

Divide Your Time by Determining Needs

One of the most respected leaders I know said, "If you're writing about sales leadership, make sure to tell leaders to use technology to their advantage but not allow it to replace them." She added that she thought loss of human contact was a primary reason why her leaders lost people.

It's an easy trap to fall into. You have a multitude of responsibilities, and it's easier, quicker, and often more practical to send an e-mail message to the team. Or you get someone's voice mail, give a brief message, and move on—relieved that you don't have to engage.

That's fine, as long as it doesn't become so much of a habit that your team begins to think their leader is a machine. Don't let it happen. Periodically make direct contact a priority. (And if you're trying to squeeze thirty-two hours into a twenty-four-hour day, reserve a little time to kick your shoes off, put your feet up, and reread chapter eight.)

How *do* you decide how to best divide your time so that those who need coaching and encouragement get it? When you start out with three or four on your team, it's a snap. You're a small, close-knit group that's ready to tackle the world. It's a lovefest, and they *all* get your attention.

But as your group grows it soon dawns on you that it's impossible to give equal time to everyone. So how do you decide who gets what when? You decide based on who needs and deserves your time most. Let's look at five profiles and see how the descriptions impact how much time you devote to each person.

The New Kid She's inexperienced and hopeful. Impact on you: She needs a considerable amount of your time, not just because she's new and green, but also because she's more open to your guidance and suggestions at this stage than she will ever be again.

The Up-and-Comer She has had moderate or little success, but she is enthusiastic, hardworking, and willing to learn. Impact on you: She needs your attention and guidance because she has that special spark you look for. She has the potential to be a top performer and move on to the next level, but she needs ongoing coaching and encouragement.

Ready to Be on Her Own She's doing exceptionally well in both selling and sponsoring. She knows the job, she's independent, and she can't wait to lead her own team. Impact on you: She needs recognition for her top performance, appreciation for her contribution, and last-minute guidance and information before you cut the cord.

Top Performer, Content Where She Is She has proven her ability through her effort and performance but wants to "do her own thing" on her schedule. (Sometimes she has a high sales performance and sometimes she chooses to do little.) She's content to stay under your wing even though you've encouraged her to go for a leadership level several times. Impact on you: She needs your recognition and appreciation, but not much else. She's a good candidate to help you train or launch new directions. (She's that steady performer you can depend on for the big pushes.) Keep your eye out for a change in either her attitude or her situation—just in case she decides to go further.

The "Now and Then Order" Kid She chooses to discount shop for personal use and gifts. She sells just the minimum the company requires to stay in business. She's made little effort and seems to like things just the way they are. Impact on you: She needs to be kept informed of changes and promotions. Again, her attitude or her personal situation may change, but unless there is a change, don't keep trying to save her from herself.

As these examples show, several variables will help you determine how best to divide your time with your team. By giving more of your attention to those who need and deserve it most, you will not only have the satisfaction of knowing you have used your time wisely, but you'll also have the comfort of knowing that if someone doesn't succeed, it's not because you weren't there for her.

Also, consider if it's possible that you tend to contact some team members more than necessary because you

- Enjoy talking with them; they're more fun and/or positive.
- Relate to them; you have much in common.
- Tend to rely on their skills and their confidence. (It's okay to learn from them, just don't become dependent on them.)

If your answer was "guilty" to any of the three, think about making some changes so that those who need, want, and deserve more of your time get it. As I wrote this, a touching story came to mind.

A mother was asked, of her five children, which was her favorite. Her answer was, "The one who is sick until he is well. The one who is away until she is home."

Be Ready for the Big Time

You've planned your time based on your team's individual needs and you have your act together at home, and then all of a sudden something glorious happens. Your team has phenomenal growth. Suddenly you're in the big league. When your business has taken off, be ready to really let go. Rita Davenport said, "If it doesn't take personality, I don't do it." She was being a bit facetious, but the message was clear. Don't waste your talents doing routine stuff like filing, stamping, making routine calls, simple errands, or housework—stuff that could be done by others. Free up that time so you can focus on those actions that have the most impact on your business. Most of those should involve *human contact,* because the continuing success of your business is in direct proportion to the attention you give to your customers and your team.

QUICK RECAP

- Get to know each person on your team so you can learn how to best motivate and guide them.

- Be specific when giving praise—always. Spell out the *why*.

- Make sure your team members sense your high energy and optimism whenever you communicate with them.

- Learn each person's personality style to better understand and reach them.

- Help team members solve their own problems so they aren't dependent on you.

- Know and practice the seven steps to coaching. You will achieve more successful outcomes.

- Don't adopt a missionary attitude—know when to cut loose a repeat offender.

- Divide your time to be there for the team members who need you.

BINDER TIME

- Take some well-invested time to answer the following questions: What do I need to learn about each person on my team? How and when will I do that? What's the best way for me to keep track of this information?

- The next time you give recognition, make sure you describe the specific action or performance that prompted it. Make note of the receiver's reaction in your binder.

- Thinking of how you coach, jot down anything you believe you can do better. What will you change based on what you just wrote? When will you make those changes?

- When the next person comes to you with a business problem, see if you can guide her to come up with her own solution. Make a note of how she reacted and how you felt about doing that.

- What can you change about your work habits that will free up more of your time so you can give the attention to those who need and deserve it most? When will you do that?

CHAPTER 12

Keeping the Troops Awake: Teaching and Holding Meetings

Although meetings and training sessions are different in many ways, the objectives of both are much the same. You want to hold the audience's attention, give clear-cut instruction or direction, and bring about a change in behavior. Let's look at both functions up close and personal.

Teach for Results

Remember what it was like in school when you had a teacher who made learning almost painful? Perhaps it was because of his monotonous tone, or his endless lecturing style. It may have been that the way he covered the information left you confused or overwhelmed rather than enlightened. Perhaps you were just plain bored and kept checking the clock to see when the torture would end. Now *you're* the teacher.

From the moment you invited the first person to join your team, your role started to change. Soon you learned that knowing how to *do* is different than knowing how to *teach.*

You start out with an advantage. Unlike schoolchildren, who learn because they have to, adults learn because they want to. (The seniors who go back to college are often more attentive and conscientious than most eighteen-year-olds.) But even though you have a receptive audience, knowing and applying key teaching principles makes it considerably easier for trainees to *get it* and *retain it!* As you read on, tick off the suggestions that prompt you to want to make some changes.

Teach New People on an "As Needed" Basis

It's easy to forget what it's like to be new and apprehensive. I always keep this saying in mind: "You never want to think like a new person, but you never want to forget how a new person thinks."

In your enthusiasm to help, or in your desire to "cover it all," you could be like a power lawn mower in a flower box and overwhelm the hapless learner.

Ask yourself these questions:

- What do they need to know and do before they start?
- What do they need to know and do the first week, the second week, etc.?

Spread out your instruction, and refer the new people to the appropriate sections of their manuals to back it up. If you haven't already done so, write up a brief training schedule for each of the initial weeks. Then you'll be sure to remember all you need to cover at a pace your trainee can absorb. The first part of this book is a valuable resource when teaching sales skills. Consider focusing on one chapter at a time to create a dynamite sales course. What a help to your team to fully grasp why people buy, the importance of stressing benefits, and when and how to close. Sure beats sending an untrained salesperson out into a trained world!

Tell Them Why

You will get adults' attention and motivate them to want to learn when you first tell them how they will benefit. Why is it important to their success to become confident closers? Why is it to their advantage to ask for referrals? Why does it make sense to keep organized, easy-to-find information about their customers? (By the way, did I tell you *why* it's important that you give them the "why"?)

Be aware that your team members learn in different ways and at different speeds. Some learn more easily by seeing a skill modeled, others by hearing about it. Some are quick learners and some are slow learners. You may think a few are out to lunch from the neck up, but it takes some people a little longer to grasp ideas or concepts. (They often end up being your stars, because once they "get it," they have it for life.) So, whether you're teaching a class or one person, mix up the way you deliver your message. Periodically ask if what you've said is clear; that way you'll know if they're still with you.

Watch facial expressions and body language. Even though trainees often have *no idea* they're doing it, their actions give them away. They grimace, get a blank stare, or begin to squirm. If you see this happening, stop and say something like, "Your face tells me I'm not explaining this very clearly."

Watch Your Speed

Speak slowly, and *pause* between subjects to allow the point you're making to sink in. In a training situation, it's easy for us to rattle on because we know the information so well. If you're guilty of speaking rapidly, most new people will get hopelessly lost and never let you know it.

Watch Your Tone

Speak at an adult level. (Former teachers and parents, beware!) If you're patronizing—your tone of voice sounds like you're speaking to a child—you risk insulting another's intelligence. This is one of my pet peeves. If you've ever had it happen to you, you know the feeling. It's not fun.

Watch Your Volume

Speak up so that those in the very back of the room can hear you loud and clear. The quiet speaker can drive listeners crazy in short order. Once the audience misses one or two key points, the whole message is down the drain. An audience will rarely tell you to speak more loudly unless you encourage it.

I finally realized that when I talk about an emotional or sensitive subject, my voice tends to drop almost to a whisper. I now ask others to tell me—loud and clear—if they can't hear me. Fortunately, they do.

Encourage Questions

Most of us are hesitant to ask questions, especially in a group. We don't want to appear dumb, and if no one else seems confused, our tendency is to sit quietly and let it pass. The risk is that you could have a room full of confused people. Encourage questions and set the stage initially. Say, "There are no dumb questions." Acknowledge what they ask in various ways:

- "That's a good question."
- "That shows you've been there before."
- "I'm so glad you asked that, because it reminds me to . . ."
- "I'm glad you asked, because I didn't make it clear that . . ."
- "That's a question I'm often asked, and it's an important one."

- "Thank you for bringing that up."
- "Hmm, that's an interesting question."

Watch that you don't get in the habit of always saying, "That's a good question"; it can soon seem contrived. The one time you *don't* say it, that person may think, "I guess mine wasn't a good question." I had someone say that to me once. We all laughed, but I got the message.

Use Open-Ended Questions

If you ask closed questions—those that can be answered with a yes or no, like, "Do you think that idea has merit?"—you'll likely get a yes, but then what? End of discussion. Open-ended questions get trainees to think. They also often open up additional areas for discussion. Here are some examples.

- "How would you handle that problem?"
- "How would you answer this question?"
- "What would you do if you found yourself in that position?"
- "Why do you think that idea has merit?"
- "When would it be appropriate to call her back, and why?"

No answer is wrong. If it's not complete or not what you want, simply say something like, "And to add to that . . ." or "Another way to approach it is . . ." It's much more tactful, and no one feels dumb!

Recognize the Value of Repetition

Have you heard the suggestion that if you want to remember someone's name, you should say it at least three times in a short time? It works because repetition helps us retain information. Remember the old adage: Tell them what you're going to tell them, tell them, tell them what you told them.

You might ask the trainees to repeat what you said, summarize the key points at the end of each segment, or refer trainees to the section in the company manual that covers the subject in a different way. If you're holding a series of classes, start the next class with a brief review of the previous class. Ask participants to share what they learned. Repetition, repetition, repetition! (Oops, I'm repeating myself.)

Tell, Show, and Critique

Whenever possible, the three-step teaching process is the best way to be assured that your instruction has been successful.

- *Tell* them what you want them to know.
- *Demonstrate* what you just told them (model it).
- *Ask* them to duplicate what you did and give them feedback (have them role-play).

The beauty of role-playing exercises is that they allow trainees to gain experience in a safe environment. They grasp what they did right, what they did wrong, and how to improve. Ah, the satisfaction that comes from imparting knowledge and feeling confident that it will be remembered—and used.

Hold Riveting Meetings

Attention to teaching skills goes beyond training. The ability to keep the troops from falling asleep on their feet is also priceless in meetings. But it can take a good deal of forethought, which can be a hard lesson to learn.

Anna, a member of my team, was a lovely and gracious senior citizen. She traveled the farthest to attend my meetings. She could be counted on to be there when others, who lived much closer, could not. What she told me after one of my meetings will be burned in my brain forever. She said, "I'm so glad I came tonight.

It was a good meeting. I had just about decided that the meetings weren't worth the long trip."

To say that comment threw me is an understatement. My first reaction was shock. I found it tough to accept that this wonderful lady could be so painfully frank. Once I straightened my nose (it was considerably "out of joint"), I realized that Anna had done me a favor. I had been under the delusion that I was holding pretty good meetings.

I asked myself what it was about that one meeting that worked for Anna. I started questioning what other leaders did. I gave the planning stage considerably more time and thought. I came up with the following guidelines. As you read through them, tick off any that you identify as your weak areas.

Set a Consistent Time and Date If at all possible, stick with the same day and time for your meetings. It's much easier for your team to keep track of and reserve dates if they know the meeting is always on the first Wednesday of the month at 7:00 PM.

Create a File Just for Meeting Ideas Cut out inspirational sayings. Look for humorous stories or cartoons that fit your business. Collect articles that will help reinforce a principle, idea, or skill. Be attuned to information in the media that's relevant to your business and worthy of passing on. Pick up on good ideas from others. When you're talking to a team member, be alert to anything she tells you that would be helpful to others. Jot it down. When someone is doing an outstanding job in a particular area, ask questions to find out why. Make an immediate note and put it in your file. If she can't attend a future meeting, relate the story or add it to a news bulletin. This not only benefits the team, it also builds the confidence of the person you singled out. You should soon have a big fat file!

Be on Top of the Details Think ahead. If you're covering dates and several details, have a handout. Use visuals, have samples, use music, whatever it takes to clarify or jazz up a presentation. Have all needed materials at your fingertips.

Start on Time No matter who's there, begin when you planned to begin. I know, this is a tough one, but those who are consistently tardy will finally get it: If they're late, they'll miss something. It's just as important to end on time. Don't keep your team more than two hours unless it's a special event.

Include Recognition, Training, Motivation, and Inspiration in General Meetings Mix up subjects with the goal of holding the group's interest. If you cover a serious subject, the next subject should be a light one. Experiment with the flow of the meeting. Once you're satisfied that you've come up with the best order, stick with it.

Get Them Up and Moving Be flexible with your agenda and watch for signs of restlessness. Call for a stretch, consider building in an activity, or have a food break.

Include Open Sharing on a Timely Subject Go around the room so *all* have a chance to participate. Depending on the subject, you might do this in the very beginning or near the end. Ask them to share a humorous experience, a valuable insight, or a new approach.

Involve Several Others Don't take on everything yourself. No matter how good you are, it's more interesting to hear different voices. The group benefits from the experiences of others, and often the message has more impact coming from a teammate. Don't be hesitant to ask a new person to help. They often have fresh insights. Although they may protest at first, they'll be flattered. And if they aren't so great the first time, they'll be better the second time. Your ongoing contact and questioning in advance will tell you whom to choose.

Train on Weak Skill Areas Select a trainer for her high performance in areas where your team is weak. Coach her to start with an attention-getting introduction, and then ask her to cover three or four key points, with examples. Ask her to use a brief outline. It will help her remember all she wants to say and, just as important, prevent her from rambling. From time to time, ask two trainers to speak as a team. This can result in interesting training because they will tend to play off each other. If numbers permit, select a panel to cover a subject from different perspectives.

Clarify and Reinforce Cover any changes and reinforce promotions, new product releases, and new company procedures. Make sure everyone understands. Encourage questions.

Stay in Control If someone brings up a negative subject that's not shared by the group or goes off on a tangent not relevant to your agenda, tactfully steer the conversation back on track. If it's an issue that needs to be addressed privately, promise to spend some time with that person after the meeting or the next day.

If a team member yearns to be in the spotlight and continually has something to say, tactfully ask for opinions or suggestions from others.

Aim for a relaxed, open, and fun environment. If you sense the meeting is slipping away, bring it back to your agenda. Your team will respect you for it. (Never allow yourself to be like the high school substitute teacher whose class took over while she looked on—helplessly.)

Challenge Them End the meeting by giving the group a challenge. Let them know that you'll ask them to talk about their experiences and insights regarding the challenge at the next meeting. (You might send a quick e-mail in between.)

End on a Positive Note Send them away on a high note. Share, or ask a team member to share, an inspirational quotation or story. If appropriate, hand out small gifts or reminders to take home.

Your meetings are your *only* chance to connect with several team members at one time. To make them pay off, take the time to think through what will best help them, inspire them, motivate them, and hold their interest. Always look to making your meetings better and better. Take a brief time after the meeting to analyze what worked and why, what didn't work and why, and what you will change the next time around.

If you're *really* courageous, give out a questionnaire asking what they liked, didn't like, and what they suggest you change or add in future meetings. Only do this if you're ready for candid answers—'cause the truth sometimes "hoits." Tell them not to sign their names. (Assure them that you won't study the handwriting either.) Do this, and you'll never hear a painful message like the one I heard from dear Anna.

The Special Case of Telephone Conferencing

Today's direct sales leaders deal with two challenges more than ever: distance and lack of time. (It's common for some team members to live hundreds, maybe even thousands, of miles away from you.) Teleconferencing has been the miracle solution for solving both problems when it comes to informing and training. But just as with any great solution, if conferencing isn't handled wisely, it can lose much of its effectiveness. Advance preparation and strong facilitation skills are a *must*. Let's tackle the issue with a dos and don'ts list.

Do

- Make it clear exactly when and how to join the call.
- Specify the time involved, allowing a small cushion of time for the unexpected.
- Cover the objectives in advance. If it's to inform, give an agenda. If it's to train, give the subject(s) to be covered and the credentials of the trainer(s).
- Ask callers to block out the specific time in a place that will be free of background interruptions.

- Advise callers in advance if there will be a Q&A.
- Ask callers to identify themselves initially when they make comments or ask questions to make it clear who's talking.

Don't

- Allow any one caller to monopolize the conversation. If this should happen, tactfully ask for input from others on the call.
- Let participants steer the conversation off course. If there's a question or concern not relevant to the call, make arrangements to speak one-on-one at a later time.
- Allow time to slip away without accomplishing the goal of the conversation. If you feel this starting to happen, remind participants of what is yet to be covered.

After the call, send an e-mail reviewing key points and decisions.

A Quick Word About Three-Way Calling

Three-way calling is a neat way to teach new people how to handle various phone skills by modeling in a real life situation. It's an ideal way to teach a trainee how to set an appointment with a prospective recruit, book a presentation, or handle a sticky situation by phone. It's an additional service with the phone company, but well worth the small cost when you're leading a team.

QUICK RECAP

- Learn to teach in a way that holds students' attention and assures that they "get it."
- Involve students in the learning process.
- Plan your meetings so that those who attend feel they're worth the time and energy.
- Know what it takes to hold an interesting and informative meeting.

- Determine the best format and time and day for the meeting and stick with it.
- Learn how to use conference calling effectively.
- Remember the value of three-way calling when modeling phone skills.

BINDER TIME

- What have you learned about teaching one-on-one that works for you?
- What have you learned about group training that works for you?
- Write down two things you can change to help you teach more effectively. Make those changes the next time you teach.
- Be brave. Tape your next meeting or training session. Then *listen to all of it* and decide if anything you heard needs improving. Write those insights in your binder.
- If you discovered any holes in the planning stages of your meetings, what are they, and how can you avoid them in the future?
- If you ticked off any suggestions you need to apply to your meetings, write them down.
- Determine specifically what you will change at your next meeting to address them.
- Jot down how those changes affected your meeting.
- If you have yet to use conference calling as a meeting or training tool, determine if it's a feasible alternative and if so, the best resources for getting up to speed.
- If it's a go, when will you use it? Write the date in your binder.

CHAPTER 13

Become Master of the Details

It's no secret that there's more to leading a team than the prestige, awards, and bouquets. That's the fun stuff. But you're heading a business. You have several responsibilities that don't get the *glory* and are likely not nearly as much fun, but that contribute considerably to your success. This chapter's all about the nitty-gritty, the details of running a business.

Keep Up with the Times

For just a moment, let me to tell you what it was like in the "good old days." (No, I won't say I walked five miles barefoot to school in a snowstorm.) When I first became a leader, I had three ways to communicate with my team: (1) face to face, (2) by mail, and (3) by phone (the kind attached to the wall—my "mobile phone" was a neck-strangling twenty-five-foot cord).

We did have answering machines, although they were not as sophisticated as today's. Other technology existed, but either it wasn't practical for home-based businesses or it wasn't in general use. What's available to me today is mind-boggling. (And even as I type, young geniuses are working to improve it or make it obsolete.)

But even though today's technology is exciting and freeing, the trick for you, as a sales leader, is to know *how* and *when* to use *what*. Obviously, to compete in today's world, you must be computer literate. But don't let the ever-increasing list of other technology options spook you.

Start from Where You Are If you feel unsure about using the system or technology your company makes available to you, then becoming more comfortable with this technology should be your number one priority.

Be Attuned to what Top Leaders Are Doing Find out what technology and programs other leaders are using. Ask questions like,

- "What are the benefits?"
- "What's the cost?"
- "How long will it take me to get up to speed?"

Based on the size of your group, decide what you should know, do, or invest in next based on your business needs. When you're confident in one area, move on to the next priority.

Check Out Your Resources Depending on your skill level, you may want to attend a class, buy a book, or ask a pro for help—whether it's a "tech whiz" friend, a paid professional, or that bright sixteen-year-old at home. (Or is it a twelve-year-old? Scary!) Be open and honest. You may be surprised at how willing others will be to help you catch up.

Give Yourself Time to Get Up to Speed It's never been said that those who learn faster learn better. Remember: *Anything worth doing is worth doing badly at first.*

Although the newest and most sophisticated technology will never replace the human touch, it can help you connect with, train, motivate, and inspire your team. Push yourself out of that comfort zone and into the twenty-first century. Have the attitude of a child: Be curious. Be playful. Be daring.

A word to the wise: To all of you tech whizzes out there, I applaud you (and I'm in awe of your talents). You're the ones who love every new gizmo or program that comes along. You're bright, you're fast, and you find it's downright fun to be on top of the latest technology. The downside? You can forget to invest the larger part of your time where it counts most. You're in a *people* business; much of your growth will come through your connections with *people.* Use those glorious time-savers, but never lose sight of the fact that it's *human* contact that builds relationships, *not* technology! They need to hear your voice, see your smile, and feel your pat on the back from time to time.

Know the Numbers

Getting to know the numbers is a dull task, but it's vital to letting you know exactly what's happening in your business. If you're not on top of the numbers for each cycle, you may lose *considerable* money. Don't let it happen! Remember, the computer doesn't have a heart—it's cold and calculating, literally, and it doesn't care if you're a nice person. And the leaders of your company can't make exceptions if you're a few dollars short of the next level of compensation. If they did, that would open up a big can of snakes (*worms* wasn't dramatic enough), no matter how sad your story. If it *were* possible to change the figures or make an exception, others would expect preferential treatment, too.

So watch those group sales. If, near the end of a sales cycle, you see that your group sales are pennies or a low-dollar figure away from the next level, act. Check with the members of your immediate team to see if they need a sample, a gift, or have a small order to submit. These are orders that can be moved almost immediately. You do the same.

Never, I repeat, *never* stockpile. (No reputable company would encourage it.) How sad that some salespeople get so caught up in wanting a higher bonus or receiving top recognition that they forget there's a downside. They can end up with financial problems because they purchased huge inventories they haven't sold. Even if they *can* afford it, it may take months to sell it. (And that lowers their future personal sales considerably while they sell off purchased stock.) Plus, others may realize what they're doing and lose respect for them. If it isn't a *real* sale, it's a hollow victory.

Know Individual Performance Records If you notice that someone on your personal team will lose commission because of a small amount not ordered, let them know—posthaste. Then, so they don't depend on you in the future, remind them to be aware of their sales figures from that point on. They'll be grateful that you were looking out for them.

Also, the figures your company provides give you the information you need to guide and coach your team. They highlight, in black and white, each person's strengths and weaknesses. They tell you loud and clear where they need help.

Watch Those Personal Promotions It feels *oh-so-good* to give your team something extra for their efforts. They love you for it, and it's easier for you to promote your own gifts. And besides, sales can go up. I don't want to be a spoilsport, and I'm not about to tell you how to run your business, but I *can* make some suggestions based on what I've learned along the way.

- *Don't overlap company promotions.* When several promotions are going on at once, it confuses your team. I've seen people receive additional "stuff" based on layered promotions they didn't know about, didn't care about, or had forgotten.
- *Keep promotions simple.* If it's not easy to understand and promote, it's not a good promotion. It's no fun piecing together a complicated promotion, let alone attempting to explain it to someone else! I know; I've plowed through some.
- *Do the math.* Guesstimate the number you think will qualify. Total the profit you'll make on that number. Subtract your total cost for the promotional items. If the numbers don't indicate you'll come out way ahead, it's not a good promotion.

Don't fall into the trap of "buying sales." Once your team gets used to your habit of always throwing something in, it's tough to take it away. Interesting thing about we humans—once we're accustomed to receiving something extra, it becomes an entitlement.

Take Care with the Written Word

I received a newsletter the other day that contained valuable information, but it was written badly—*big time.* I immediately formed a negative opinion of the author. Was that fair? No, he may be a talented person, and he's probably a nice guy to boot. But I judged him by his writing. Intellectually, I know better (and my editors can verify that I'm *light years* away from perfect). But right or wrong, we're judged by how we write. What we say on paper (or electronically) represents us. So it's worth whatever it takes to be well represented.

Aim for correctly written, clear, concise messages that leave no doubt in the reader's mind regarding what you want them to know or do. Perhaps you're already a pro. If so, the following ideas will simply affirm that you're on the right track. But if writing isn't your strong suit, these suggestions are a good beginning. As before, tick off any that are your weak areas.

Be a Fanatic About Grammar and Spelling I think those who invented spell check and grammar correction deserve a place in Heaven without stopping at the gate. But *nothing* is foolproof. (And you're *really* out there in the cold when your message is handwritten.) So reread what you write before it leaves your hands or you click Send. More than once I've sent off a speedy message only to discover later that it had a typo—or several! (And there was no pushing Rewind!)

Accept That Less Is Better If you tend to be wordy, rein yourself in. As you read a sentence, if you can eliminate words without sacrificing the meaning, chop, chop away. And don't hold onto something not needed because you're emotionally attached to the wording. Be brutal!

E-mail messages are a whole different animal. They should be short and to the point: a tip of the week, reinforcement of a promotion or change, notice of an upcoming event, or brief recognition. They're ideal for reminding, informing, and appreciating your team. They're not the best medium for involved messages. (Again, they don't *replace* human contact.)

Give Yourself Time Unless it's a message that must go out immediately, wait to send it. What seems perfect the first time around is often, for many reasons, anything but. You may be tired, rushed, or distracted, so you won't be as discerning as you would be later. The eye plays tricks on us; we see what seems logical and what we meant to say no matter what we write. When we reread later, we often pick out obvious errors or confusing wording.

Check Out the Overall Look of Your Message Is it text heavy? Is there enough of a margin (white space)? If it looks overwhelming, some readers won't bother to finish reading it. You may need to continue to chop away or separate key ideas into more paragraphs. You're aiming for the text to be reader friendly, and the more it is, the better, since many of today's readers want *everything* to be quick and easy.

Learn from Others Take special note of *anything* you read that's well written and easy to understand. You may be surprised at what you can pick up by analyzing someone else's skillful writing. Perhaps the opening sentence was a real grabber. Perhaps it was that there was no mistaking what the writer wanted you to do. Perhaps the message made you smile.

I touched on the power of books earlier. Have a variety of reading material in your house. Don't sequester it to a library; place it throughout the house, especially in locations where you might have a few minutes to yourself, time that you can spend reading without interruption (if you know what I mean). Not only will you increase your vocabulary, but if you're looking for it, you'll soon discover what works and doesn't work in writing.

Be Aware of the Tone Any wording that could be perceived as a criticism is best left unwritten. What we *say* is one thing: We can use a soft tone and manner. We can see reactions. We can even amend it midsentence. What we write, however, is a permanent record.

Check for Clarity Since you're so familiar with what you want to say, your message may seem quite clear to you. However, this isn't always the case with the recipient. Read over what you write. Is there anything that could have a double meaning? Are there any words that aren't easily known and understood? If not, it's ready to go.

Check the Flow Ask yourself if the first words will catch the reader's attention. Does the first paragraph tell the reader the purpose of your message? Does each new paragraph tie in logically with the previous one?

Acknowledge Goofs Don't allow errors to go unacknowledged. We've all sent something we later regretted sending—for *whatever* reason. If it's a biggie, depending on the goof, you can send a humorous follow-up—or a serious apology. Only let it go if it's a small transgression.

Call In the Troops When I was a department head, I asked that materials be read by at least three different people before they went out to the sales force. (We all knew the risks if we didn't have this safeguard. We learned the hard way!) If you're sending an involved or critical message, get a second or third opinion. A new eye and a different perspective can spot weaknesses or errors you missed.

Get Help If you have other priorities or you simply don't like writing, find someone competent to handle the big stuff. Maybe it's a friend, a relative, or a professional. As long as what's written clearly communicates what you want to say, it doesn't matter who writes it.

A professional friend recommended I read *On Writing Well*, by William Zinsser. It's a fantastic reference book. It's packed with examples, and it's easy to understand. That shouldn't be a surprise, given the title. You may want to keep a copy close at hand. Let me make that stronger—get a copy!

QUICK RECAP

- Learn to use current technology that will help you be a more efficient and effective leader. Accept that you don't need to be perfect in the beginning.
- Make it a habit to be aware of monthly figures so that you and your immediate team don't miss out on higher compensation by a small amount.

- Don't add personal promotions that will confuse, spoil, or overwhelm your team. Make sure the projected sales justify the cost.
- Recognize that everything you write is a reflection of you.
- Aim for clear, concise writing.
- Be scrupulous when proofreading. Ask others to proofread when writing detailed information.
- Make note of anything that's written well and holds your attention. Determine why that's so.

BINDER TIME

- *Technology:* Think about what's currently being used in your field, and taking into account the size and geographic locations of your team, choose one thing that you have allowed to spook you. (Come on, there must be one.) Now, make a commitment and take that first step toward tackling it. Jot down the date you plan that step. Then schedule the next step when you've reached the first date.
- *Tech whiz kids:* Have you overused your knowledge at the expense of human contact? If you answered "guilty," nip it in the bud. What can you change that will free up more time for the human side of business? When will you do that? Jot the date in your binder.
- *Know the numbers:* Determine the best way to follow up regularly so you know exactly where you stand near the end of each cycle. (Since your appointment book is something you check daily, consider using it as a reminder, and highlight the notation in an attention-getting color.)
- *Promotions:* What was the best personal promotion you ever ran? Why do you think that was? What have you learned the hard way about personal promotions?

- Review those points you selected to improve in your writing. Determine the change you consider the most critical. Make that change immediately. Tackle any others as you go so that your written words do you justice.

CHAPTER 14

Team Playing: Using All Your Resources

I see her face as I write, and I'm smiling. Nancy was a born cheerleader. People lit up when she entered a room. She was funny, positive, and enthusiastic. She was one of the most loyal and loving people I have ever had the joy of knowing.

Whenever we were stretching to make a team goal, it was Nancy who rallied the troops. When the team needed a pep talk, it was Nancy who gave it. (I didn't even have to ask.) And although she may never have known it, it was Nancy's positive outlook and beautiful spirit that kept me going through some tough times. Thank you, Nancy.

Barbara was my conscience. She was analytical, fair, and wise. She was highly respected by her fellow teammates. As a senior member of the team, she was the one I looked to when I was wrestling with a team-issue question. She was always tactful. Yet I knew I could trust that she would tell me exactly what she thought. Thank you, Barbara.

It was said that Walt Disney couldn't draw well enough to get a job in his own studio. Yet he was a sterling example of effective leadership, not only because he had an incredible vision and high expectations, but also because he knew his team's strengths—and how to bring out the best in them.

When you're confident about who you are, you can rely on others without feeling threatened. You don't need to have all the answers. You don't need to be everything to everybody. Here again is why it's so valuable to be aware of team members' individual strengths. When you tap those strengths, you have collective knowledge and collective power! In this case, one plus one equals three, or maybe even four.

Thinking of your team members, determine who's the

- Most empathetic, caring one
- Detail person, the organizer
- Most effervescent, positive one—the one to rally the team
- Analytical problem solver
- Most technology savvy

That's only five strengths. Imagine the wealth of talent, knowledge, and experience that's right there in front of you. Are you using this killer resource to reach team goals? Do you solve problems as a team? Do you work on creative approaches as a team? Can you think of a team member who could help you with a current project or challenge? Could there be others whose abilities you may have underestimated—or just not tapped? Tell them you need their skills and watch them shine!

Have a Vision—a Dream

The power of teams to accomplish big things is directly related to the vision, courage, and fortitude of the leader. The impressive stories of legendary leaders are endless. Imagine for a moment the impact the following five leaders had on their followers—and on society: Susan B. Anthony and women's suffrage, Jack Welch and GE, Steve Jobs and Apple, Katherine Graham and the *Washington Post*, and Mary Kay Ash and Mary Kay Cosmetics.

Getting outstanding sales-team results starts with your belief in yourself as a leader and your faith in your team's ability. If you tend to come up with those infamous "buts" in your head, you're dead in the water. You know, "We *could* do much more, *but*_____."

The blank space can be filled in with anything you think limits your team's possibilities. The more "buts" you come up with, the more likely it is that you won't see much growth. But by changing just two words, *everything* changes: "We *can* do much more *because*___."

What your team accomplishes is a direct result of what you *think* they can accomplish. That may sound simplistic, but it's true. So, think beyond the now and make it a big stretch. You've got to believe what you want to accomplish is possible. If you don't, they won't.

Help Them Grow Closer

The more team members know each other, the closer they'll become; the closer they become, the more they'll function as a cohesive, supportive group.

Periodically, write up a special in-depth profile of a team member or spotlight her at a meeting. Your team will discover things they respect and admire about others who they only knew superficially before. Send a brief biography by e-mail whenever you introduce a new member. End it with: "I know you look forward to meeting and welcoming Sylvia in person at (next event)."

Divide your immediate team into small groups to brainstorm or to work on a joint project. Comparative strangers can become a close-knit group in no time when they're working together on a mutual goal.

There's nothing much more moving than seeing team members care as much about what they accomplish *together* as what they accomplish individually. And as their leader, you'll have the satisfaction of knowing you created the climate that made it happen.

Celebrate Every Step Forward

To help your team stay energized and optimistic, consistently make them aware of positive movement or growth. It helps them feel the team power that unites and inspires them.

Any progress is a reason to reward them. It needn't be anything extravagant. One leader gave out thirteen-inch rulers as a symbol of growth. Another gave engraved pencils with the team's slogan. I once distributed candy bars with a tag attached that read: "How sweet it is!"

You might simply write a heartfelt note, send a touchy-feely e-mail, or create a certificate. If it's a big accomplishment, and it's feasible, consider a picnic, a breakfast get-together, or a pizza party. Not only are these celebrations fun, but they also draw team members closer to you and each other. Make sure to include spouses. As one top sales leader said, "Winning spouses over was a major coup—and it saved more than one team member."

Consider a Master Plan

Once you can see beyond the *now* and can start visualizing an outstanding future, you're ready to get the team involved. This is when your energy and optimism are sorely needed—*it's your power!*

Just telling your team what you think they can accomplish won't cut it. *Together,* you need to come up with a well-thought-out plan that defines where you want to go and how you're gonna get there. With a plan agreed on by all, everyone's focused and dedicated to the outcome. Then the *team's* energy and creativity will take over.

I've outlined one way to rally your team and accomplish big things. If you decide to give it a try, it will take time, thought, and perseverance, but the end result could be impressive. Look it over. If it's a fit for you and your team, then the next question is, Is the time right? If you get two yeses, sleep on it before moving on it.

GOING FOR IT

When you decide to tackle a long-range goal it requires the team's enthusiastic acceptance of that goal and their willing participation in achieving it. You'll want to set the stage in advance by arousing their curiosity and letting them know that what you'll be proposing is a "big deal." The following is the way to do just that:

- Call a special meeting.
- Give plenty of notice so more team members can attend.
- Let your team know the meeting will take longer than usual. Specify the hours.
- Plan to serve something unexpected and special.
- Promote it—big time. Let them know you're counting on them. You might send humorous messages that arouse their curiosity. Here's an example: "Are you ready for a stretch? No, I don't mean at the gym. I have a challenge for you—the collective you. Show up on _____, at _____, for a _____ hour special meeting. And we'll see if you, the team, really has the stuff I'm convinced you have! Curious? Good! That was my goal. PS: Rest up the night before; you'll want to be alert!"

This Going for It example follows my style; it may not be yours. The purpose of the example is to stimulate your thinking. After you send the first message, send post cards or reminders by e-mail or text message. You might write things like "Hope you're feeling creative," or "Hope you're feeling confident." The objective is to build curiosity.

Before the Meeting

Since you'll need several things written on the flip chart during the meeting, you might ask one or two people to be your recorders in advance of the date.

Write the following headings on eight separate pages. Fill out pages one and two before the meeting. Display page one and *reveal* pages two through eight as you go.

Use the following page headings:

1. "Thought for the Day" (write your favorite inspirational saying)
2. "My Vision, My Dream: I'm convinced we can (specific goal) by (date)"
3. "Positive Adjectives That Describe Our Team"
4. "Team Statistics for the Last _____" (whatever time period you think appropriate)
5. "The Actions We Need to Take to Meet Our Goal"
6. "Mile Markers to Show We're on Pace"
7. "Ways We Can Support Each Other"
8. "Our Slogan"

Once you have put the appropriate headings on each page, you're ready to roll.

At the Meeting

Once the formalities and greetings are over, tell your team how you feel about them and why you believe they have considerable untapped potential. Then state the purpose of the meeting.

Next, flip to page two and take it from there. (You have much to cover, so stay focused and stay on track.)

Page Two Get the team's agreement regarding the goal and date. If they don't believe it's possible, they won't be wholeheartedly behind it. It's only a go when everyone accepts it. Encourage comments. Be open to negotiation *only* if you get big-time resistance. (Often the strong will bring along the unconvinced.)

Page Three Ask them to list every positive adjective they can think of that describes the team. Remind them that it's these strengths that will make it happen. (Don't help with the list till they're finished coming up with several adjectives.)

Page Four Review team statistics: sales, new people, and promoted leaders. Point out the areas that need improvement. You may choose to review the previous six months or the entire previous year. The length of time you cover depends on how long you have been a leader.

Page Five Ask your team to come up with the specific actions they need to take to reach the goal. Tap their creativity. Encourage them to think outside the rectangle. Aim for several suggestions. Add them to the chart.

Page Six Decide "mile markers"—specific increases in increments—for sales, new people, or promoted leaders that will lead them to the ultimate goal. The mile markers might be by the week or the month. Add them to the chart. (Consider asking an artistic person on your team to create a poster for a future meeting.)

Page Seven Once they agree on actions and mile markers, ask them how they can support and encourage each other. Then, tell them how you plan to support and encourage them. You guessed it: Add all that information to the chart.

Page Eight Together you may want to create a slogan, something that helps the team stay inspired and united. (You may be surprised when even the most sophisticated team members "catch the spirit.")

An easy way to select a slogan without hurting anyone's feelings is to ask each person to write a suggestion on a sheet of paper (which you provide). Once you collect them, write them all on the chart. Then ask each attendee to vote for the slogan they like most. You might want to delay this exercise, have them think on it, and bring their suggestions to the next meeting.

Wrap up the discussion by painting the picture of how it will feel once they reach their team goal. Describe the excitement of the recognition and their pride in the accomplishment. If you need inspiration on this one, check out Affirmations in chapter one. (It would be wise to write this out in advance so that it has the impact you want.)

Note: You'll want to inform those who could not attend of the results of the meeting and encourage them to "join the team."

Evaluate, Inform, Adjust (EIA) Stay on top of the numbers. As with any team goal, let the team know how they're doing on a regular basis. You may need to change their focus based on how they're progressing. Your upbeat attitude and can-do spirit will keep them going. Remember: *never* create a vision without giving ongoing updates, support, and encouragement.

Developing Leaders

There's nothing much more rewarding, exciting, and profitable than developing other leaders. If you have already done so, you're likely nodding your head in agreement. If you have yet to promote someone, this one's *especially* for you.

I've heard seemingly endless poignant stories of people who have grown both professionally and personally because someone believed in them—often long before they believed in themselves. I've seen top performers stand on stage in tears and thank their leaders for their faith and support.

I look back on my career (actually, my life), and as if by magic, a fairy godperson (FGP) appeared when I needed one, often just in the nick of time. They recognized my strengths. They believed in me. They pushed me out of my comfort zone. (It happened again with this book.)

I'm betting that you also have a FGP, likely several. Well, now you're in the position to be one! But even if you're confident in your ability to develop leaders, it helps to be reminded of the key behaviors that explain why some are more adept at it than others.

J. Sterling Livingston wrote an outstanding article in the *Harvard Business Review* on this very subject titled "Pygmalion in Management." Using in-depth research results, the author drew the following four conclusions regarding managers who lead teams with high achievers.

1. The manager's high expectations had a huge influence on a subordinate's performance. (Although the manager's expectations were high, the subordinate did not perceive them as out of reach.)

2. New subordinates were much more influenced by the manager's words and guidance. (They had yet to develop habits or attitudes that could hold them back.)

3. The manager sincerely believed in the subordinate's ability to do well. (If the manager tried "faking it," the subordinate sensed it.)

4. The manager was confident in his or her own ability to develop others. (This is the *key* component often left out in discussions and articles regarding developing others.)

Although this thesis was based on an employee-employer relationship, the same principles apply to self-employed followers. Throughout this book I've stressed the importance of your belief in your ability. The same is true when it comes to developing others. It starts with your belief that you can, because it's this belief that gives power to what you say.

> *Good is the enemy of great!*
> —JIM COLLINS, AUTHOR OF *Good to Great*

Drop Hints Early On From the beginning, point out the financial advantages of going for a leadership role even when the new person's initial goal is to have a part-time business. It's not unusual to see today's part-timer turn into tomorrow's superstar. Don't let what they say they want stop you from letting them know what they could have.

Often, fear and lack of confidence are the reasons new people hesitate initially. It's a safety net. They think they can't fail if they don't try. Give them *your* confidence. Help them tap *their* courage. Let them know you sincerely believe they have the potential to accomplish *whatever* they choose to accomplish. Emphasize their strengths, expect them to do well, and encourage them to continually move out of their comfort zone. And when you recognize each small success and continue to reinforce your belief that they can go further, they begin to believe it, too.

Guide them, little by little. Help them identify their weak areas, then, step by step, teach them to become proficient in each of those areas. (Here's where your coaching skills come into play.)

Fill Them In on the Nitty-gritty Immediately before they're on their own, cover any specifics that will make their transition to leadership easier. (Are there any small details you wish you had known in advance? If so, make sure to pass them on.) There should be no surprises.

There's *Always* a Connection Let those you promote know that you aren't about to go away. (Perhaps initially there are some things you can do jointly.) Keep in touch by sending a card, note, or e-mail. If you have an insight or a new idea, pass it on. Express your pride in their growth.

As you continue to see both professional and personal growth in your new leaders, remember that without your guidance, praise, and belief in them, it may never have happened. Pat yourself on the back for a job well done.

Accept Setbacks

I know it takes considerable time and emotional energy to develop others. Every once in a while—*through no fault of your own*—a potential leader will say she's changed her mind. How do you roll with that setback? I couldn't say it better than one top sales executive, who has developed many leaders, said it: "I learned this the hard way. I would be devastated if someone I truly believed in, someone I dreamed big dreams with, backed out. I finally accepted that it happens, it's not my fault, and it's always better to have two or three to dream with at the same time."

QUICK RECAP

- Know and use the strengths of your team to accomplish what would be difficult or impossible on your own.
- Help the team grow closer by finding ways for them to get to know each other better.
- Celebrate each victory so your team gains a sense of power.
- Focus on what the team *can* do and *why*, rather than what they can't do.

- *You* must have a vision and believe it's possible before your team can see it and believe it's possible.
- Consider working with your team to develop a master plan for exceptional growth.

BINDER TIME

- What leader rallies her team and accomplishes tough team goals consistently?
- Would it be of value to ask her for advice? (If yes, when will you ask?)
- What team members would jump at the chance to help you launch a "thinking bigger" campaign?
- Who can you count on to keep others going?
- Are there team members whose strengths you haven't called on? If so, list their names and corresponding strengths.
- How will you utilize those strengths in the future?
- Is there anything you're doing, or *not* doing, that's hampering your team's growth? If so, how can you change that?
- When the next new team member comes on board, will you do anything differently? If so, what?
- Pick out three members of your team and list a particular strength for each. How would that strength be a benefit when leading others?
- Do you believe that you have the ability to develop several future leaders? If so, why do you think that is? If not, where will you go for help?

CHAPTER 15

Handling the Bumps in the Road

It's one thing to be optimistic; it's another to be *realistic*. From time to time you'll need to handle touchy situations that require you to "think on your feet." Wise leaders know it helps to keep in mind the end result they want and to know what to do to get there. Let's look at four challenges you might be faced with and how to handle them.

Say! Who Motivates the Motivator?

You're constantly giving to others, encouraging and inspiring them, and all that other good stuff. But what keeps *you* going? Who picks you up when you feel like you're losing that fire in your belly? One question leaders have often asked over the years is, "Who motivates the motivator?" The answer? Go into the bathroom, stand at the sink, and look straight ahead. There's your answer! All right, enough of my being a Smart Alice.

The obvious answer is that *you* motivate the motivator. You're the one who knows when you need to give yourself a pep talk, get help, or simply take a break. You know what to do. The question is, do you do it? Or do you try faking it and hope that "downer feeling" goes away all by itself? Sometimes it *will* go away, but if it doesn't, you'll want to do something about it.

You need to stay motivated not only because it keeps *you* going, but also because it impacts your team. If that spark isn't there, you can bet it won't be long before they'll pick up on it, and that can affect their morale—big time! So if you find you need a shot in the arm or a boot in the pants, consider the following:

- Remind yourself of *why* you're working. Sometimes we can get so involved (or overwhelmed) that we can forget to renew our enthusiasm by reminding ourselves of the positive end results we're going for.

- Recognize how far you've come. You might list all the positive changes, personal and professional, that are a direct result of your career choice. It might be even *more* enlightening to create a before-and-after list. (If you have a family, you might get them involved.)

- Seek out inspirational renewal. It can be a tape, a book, or a person you admire—someone who has weathered more than most and still sees the glass as half full.

- If finances permit, check out a seminar you might attend. I have had the opportunity to hear some of the best inspirational speakers, and their messages have been uplifting and sustaining. I've come home renewed and rededicated.

- Ask those with staying power how they do it. You might be surprised to find that you are not alone and you'll discover one or two ideas you hadn't thought of.

- Take a break. It doesn't need to be a formal vacation. Tell your team (and your family) that you're not available for a few days. If you have young children, find a good buddy or relative who can spell you. Believe it or not, the world will *not* fall apart if you hide for a couple of days.

A dear friend, a successful business leader, periodically holes up in a hotel overnight, orders room service, and reads what could be called a "zero value" novel. She's then ready to take on the world again!

You might consider a weekend religious or nature retreat. When you have the luxury of silence, you'll be able to think clearly again and come back renewed. In the meantime, find an activity that renews you. It can be gardening, playing with the dog, reading a captivating novel, walking in a beautiful neighborhood you have never visited before, or treating yourself to a massage. *Anything* that makes you smile or takes your mind off business helps. Remember that "well" you keep dipping into for others? You need to fill it now and then, or it will *surely* run dry.

Know Where Your Responsibilities Start and End

It's an easy trap. Your team trusts you and they know you care about them. After all, you do all those good things we talked about: You cheer them on, you coach them, you inspire them, and besides all that, you're a good listener! So if a team member is struggling with a personal problem, it's understandable if she turns to you for advice. You're a problem solver, so it's equally understandable if you want to give it. However, you are *not* your team's psychologist, pastor, rabbi, very best friend in the world, or parent. Don't go there.

There are many potential risks if you and a team member blend the boundaries between your professional and personal lives.

- Becoming a counselor is time consuming, and there are many other priorities begging for your time—including a personal life.

- Listening to personal problems is emotionally draining. The tears soak in, so you often end up absorbing another's sadness.

- When you hear only one side, you could easily give the wrong advice.

- Even if you give great advice, it may come back to haunt you. An involved party may get upset. Or once everything's hunky-dory, well-intentioned you could end up being the heavy.

- Forgive my bluntness, but juicy as some of the stuff may be, it's none of your business.

You are their business friend, *not* their confidant. Should you find yourself in this sticky situation, say something like: "You know I care about you, and I sure wish I could help, but I can't. I know how to support you in your business, but this is way over my head." Then suggest she consider seeking the advice of a close friend, relative, or professional. If you're *already* in the muck and mire, tactfully dig your way out—now!

Handling a Conflict with a Peer

It would be nice to believe that everybody will always get along and all relationships with peers will be peachy keen. We know better. That's not the real world. So if you have a conflict with a peer, it's far better to confront it than to build up resentment or talk behind the offender's back.

But first, be *sure* that what bugs you isn't something petty that should just be ignored. After all, we don't always like those we work with, and they don't always like us. (I know, that second part is hard to believe.) The best way to determine whether to do something or not about this sort of situation is to ask yourself if the person's actions truly hamper you (or your team) in business. If the answer is yes, *then* act.

Depending on the severity of the problem, you may need to consult with a leader in your company or ask them to mediate.

If at all possible, it's better for two professionals to be able to "talk it out" and come to an amiable agreement. You'll notice that in many ways the following suggestions are similar to coaching.

- Know in advance what you will say, and even though it may not happen, be prepared for the other person to get defensive. Be determined to stay calm, friendly, and open to what the offender has to say. If at all possible, meet face-to-face. Thank the person for their time, and after brief small talk, get to the point. You might say something like, "I'm sure we both want to be able to work well together, but there's something that's bothering me and getting in the way of our relationship. I knew if we could talk it out, we could work it out."

- Describe the specific action that's causing the problem. Describe the negative effect on you or your team. Hear what the other person has to say. Paraphrase it so you're sure you got it.

- Be open-minded. You may learn something that will help you see things in a different light. Together, discuss ways to eliminate the problem in the future. Go for an acceptable compromise. End on a positive note by expressing your desire for a good working relationship and shake hands.

Does it always go smoothly? No, but often it does when you're prepared, when you go into the meeting with an open mind, and when you're willing to hear the other person out. Plus, you have the satisfaction of knowing that you handled a touchy situation with class.

Separate That Rare Bad Apple

Every once in a while, someone comes along who can undermine a whole team by being untruthful, manipulative, disloyal, or just plain mean. Hopefully, you won't ever have to deal with this kind of problem, but if you do, you need to take action promptly. But before you do *anything* . . .

- Make sure you can describe the specific action or behavior as seen by you and/or others. You may want to document this. Remember, it can't be an opinion, hunch, or hearsay.

- Determine if it's an ethical problem or against company policy. If it goes against company policy, consult with your company leader to determine your options if the behavior doesn't change.

- Expect the person to be defensive. Decide what you will say and how you will act in the worst-case scenario. Your goal is to be clear, calm, focused, and in control of the situation—no matter how the other person responds. And if you've thought it through, you will be.

- Take action: (1) meet face-to-face; (2) describe the specific behavior causing the problem; (3) describe the specific negative impact, first on the individual, then on others or the company; (4) listen to and acknowledge her response; (5) spell out the consequences if the behavior doesn't stop; (6) ask for a commitment that the behavior will end immediately; and (7) express your desire to continue the relationship based on the agreed-upon changes.

There are some absolutes to keep in mind during the meeting. Your goal is to stay on track, keep your cool, stay in control, and avoid saying anything that could make an uncomfortable situation worse. Use the following points as a guideline.

- Be conscious of keeping your tone calm, confident, and serious. It sets the stage for the conversation.
- Never use words that are a personal attack. It's not, "You're a liar!" It's, "You told me this and this is how I learned it wasn't so."
- Don't be apologetic or attempt to say nice things to soften the message. It will only confuse the issue.
- Stick to the subject. When someone is being confronted regarding an unacceptable behavior, a common defense is to point out the faults of others or attempt to change the subject. Don't allow yourself to be sidetracked. If this happens, simply state that you need to bring the conversation back to the purpose of the meeting. For example: "The purpose of this conversation is to discuss_____. I need to keep us focused on that."
- Make sure your tone conveys concern, not contempt.

When you know how to handle emotional and sensitive situations and can keep your cool, you're halfway there. That's what leadership is all about.

QUICK RECAP

- Be quick to notice if your motivation is slipping away.
- Take action to turn it around so it doesn't have a negative effect on you or your team.
- Recognize the risks of getting involved with team members' personal problems.
- Tactfully remove yourself from the role of counselor when you see that happening.
- If you have a conflict with a peer, make sure it's a justifiable complaint.
- Know what you will say and how you will say it.

- Be open to hearing their side.
- Go for a win-win by discussing compromises.
- End on a positive note.
- When a team member has stepped over the line with unacceptable or unethical behavior, plan to act immediately.

  - Check out your options for handling the situation before you meet.
  - Keep your tone neutral.
  - Steer the conversation where you want it to go.
  - Expect defensiveness or evasion, and be ready to handle either.
  - Require an acceptable solution.

BINDER TIME

- Have you ever found your motivation waning? If so, what did you do about it?
- What advice appealed to you most?
- Has your relationship with any team member gone from business friend to personal counselor? If so, how can you change that without hurting the business relationship? When will you do that?
- Have you had a conflict with a peer? If so, how did you handle it? What were the results?
- Have you ever had to confront someone for unacceptable or unethical behavior? If so, how did it feel? What was the result?
- What suggestions or advice in particular got your attention? Make a note of what they were so you will remember them should you need them in the future.

CHAPTER 16

But Wait—There's More!

I get a kick out of those commercials where the spokesperson offers a product at a bargain, and then to entice viewers to act immediately, throws in two or three more products for free. I know the "But wait! There's more!" line is coming every time, and I still laugh.

When I first wrote the outline for this book, I created headings that I thought would cover all I wanted to say. Then I'd find myself thinking of something that didn't fit in any particular category, but something I still felt compelled to share—just from me to you. Other times I had an enlightening experience and knew immediately that I wanted to tell you about it. That's the purpose of this last chapter.

The following are some thoughts and experiences from throughout my life that have helped me along the way.

Keep Your Eye on the Journey If you see sales as a matter of winning or losing or as an ongoing struggle, you not only won't have much fun, but you can also get discouraged and just give up. If you see what you do as an exciting challenge to your ingenuity and ability, you will find joy in the doing.

Love the Struggle I recently attended the largest poetry festival in the United States. Although I know little about poetry, it was time well spent. I was in awe of the gathering of incredibly talented poets, and moved by their beautiful readings. I was equally impressed by the attentiveness and appreciation of the audience. (Some had made long trips, and we all sloshed through muddy grounds on a bone-chilling, miserable, damp day.)

I was blown away by the speakers' obvious love for what they do. One nationally known poet was asked how he felt when nothing came to him, when he hit a dry spell. His said his favorite quotation was, "The thing that makes us happy is to be absorbed in a task that is difficult." Nuff said.

Give It Away I've been blessed to have several mentors over the years. One special gentleman, Gordon Shave, had a profound impact on my life. He taught me how to facilitate small group training, but I learned *much* more from Gordon. To me he was the great "I am." He told me that someday I might be the great "I am," and that if I were, I should always be willing to give it away.

Sometimes, it's tough to give others what we've discovered the hard way, to share the secrets of our success. But as my beloved father-in-law often said regarding taking the right path: "It's the thing to do."

Look Straight Ahead You're in competition with only one person—*yourself*. The goal is to "better your best." That way, each little step, each move outside your comfort zone, is a victory to be celebrated. Be like the horse with blinders. You may just end up way out front.

Make It Definite Know the difference between "I'll try" and "I intend." When you say you'll try (either to yourself or others), it's almost a sure bet that you won't. It's a subtle but telling sign that you lack commitment. What you "intend" is specific. It's a plan, a goal. People with high intention know what they want, and they're determined to achieve it. Another way to put it is, What you intend is what you get.

Recognize the Imposters When you're at the very top of your game you can lose perspective and see yourself as the "greatest that ever lived." When you're at the very bottom, you can see yourself as someone with little worth. As a kid, I loved the poem "If" by Kipling. These two lines have stayed with me for many years:

If you can meet with triumph and disaster
And treat those two imposters just the same

My interpretation is that when all is going magnificently, I'm to be in touch with my humility. When everything is going to heck in a bucket, I'm to be in touch with my self-worth.

Accept That You're Human If you do something dumb, be the first to see the humor in it. Sometimes we're so busy protecting our fragile egos that we give our goofs way too much power over us. I love the plaque hanging in my guest room: "Blessed are we who can laugh at ourselves, for we shall never cease to be amused."

Learn to Be in the Now I'd be ashamed to tell you how many times I've messed up on this one. I've been surrounded by the beauty of nature, in the company of dear friends, or having what should have been a fun-filled day, yet most of the joy of the moment was lost because I was there in body only. My mind was somewhere else— usually on work issues, upcoming business events, reports, etc.

When you could be joyful and relaxed but instead your mind is wandering off to Business World USA, say to yourself, "Be here now!" Focus on what's around you and take it all in. I wear a bracelet to remind me. It reads, "Nothing is more important than this day."

Make It a Sunny Day After a long gray winter, I was *ready* for a warm, clear, sunshiny day. Yesterday was that kind of day. I felt almost giddy. I had spring fever—big time.

I was also feeling deliciously lazy. The last thing I wanted to do was go grocery shopping, but I was out of dog food, and the only thing worse than no dog food in my home is no dishwashing soap.

I noticed the large display of spring plants at the entrance to the store. It was a perfect day for buying flowers. I initiated a conversation with a fellow shopper. We both admitted we had "black thumbs." We laughed as we compared failures and finally decided to choose hearty geraniums. We agreed that at least *they* had a shot at making it past a month.

In the store I saw an adorable child with several neat cornrows. I told her I *loved* her hair. She smiled from ear to ear and ran giggling to her mother.

As I was leaving the parking lot, a young woman drove up in a new mint-green Acura. I commented that it was one beautiful car. She beamed and thanked me. (That comment probably eased the pain of those monthly payments.)

I drove down an unfamiliar street and saw an elderly woman on the porch soaking up the sun. I slowed down and yelled out the window: "How wonderful to be able to enjoy sunshine for a change." She responded loud and clear: "Sure beats spring cleaning."

By now, no way did I want to go home. Fortunately, I hadn't bought ice cream, so I stopped at the park and walked for about a mile. I read every plaque on the many benches donated in memory of loved ones. I thought, *What a touching tribute—a bench in the park.* I smiled at everyone passing by. It was almost as if I couldn't help myself. *To the person*, they smiled back or made a friendly comment.

Perhaps those I greeted were more open to my warm overtures because it was a beautiful day. But my guess is that my obvious joyfulness and willingness to reach out rubbed off. I promised myself

I'd be joyful on the next cloudy day. Think about it, have you made it a sunny day lately?

Be Mindful of the Kindness of Strangers Over time, I've had many strangers take the time to help me. I've had someone retrieve a dropped package before I could even move to pick it up. I've had someone hold the door for me, often when I was still several feet away. I've had someone help me up the stairs with a heavy suitcase. The list goes on and on. But I had one experience that will stay with me for a long time.

I was wandering around a huge parking lot, desperately looking for my car. To make it worse, it was unusually warm and humid and I had a cart full of groceries.

I must have been a sorry sight. A couple about to pull away saw my dilemma and offered to help. I described my car and they insisted on driving up and down several rows of cars to see if they could find it.

Several minutes later they returned smiling and waving. They were sure they had spotted it. When they pointed it out I didn't have the heart to tell them it wasn't my car. They had already spent a good deal of time driving around. They smiled and waved goodbye.

An older gentleman was watching the show. He said it was getting dark and that it wasn't a safe area. He insisted on staying till I found my car. Finally, I located it! I yelled, "Bingo!" across the lot. He yelled back, "Great!" and drove away.

The message? It's easy these days to become somewhat cynical and hardened. We're bombarded daily with horror stories concerning man's inhumanity to man. Appreciating and remembering the little kindnesses we experience (and there are many) reminds us that there *is* much good in the world and that it's okay to have faith in others. I have this theory that the more we *expect* goodness, the more we *find it* all around us.

Remember the Other Fellow As we gain confidence and success, it can be an easy trap to become enamored with ourselves. Accolades and awards are powerful stuff. We start believing our own headlines—even when it's yesterday's news. We start focusing on the "me" and forget the "you." I love this funny line spoken by Bette Midler in the movie *Beaches*: "But enough about me. What do you think about me?"

Hold fast to your concern and interest in others—their needs, their challenges, their dreams, what they think, and what they have to say. Not only will you continue to learn, you will also never lose touch with what *really* matters—relationships.

Stretch and Grow When I was younger, much of my focus was on increasing my income, getting a title, and "making it," whatever that meant. Anytime I stretched in a new direction, it was business related: What could I learn from this course? How would this new direction help me in business? When I got older, I "settled in." I socialized mostly with old friends and tended to shy away from new experiences. I found enormous comfort in sameness.

I now realize that *only* by stretching out, in even the smallest ways, will I continue to grow and experience this thing called living. I recognize that new experiences can lead me in exciting new directions and allow me to meet fascinating new people. A friend called the other day and during our conversation dropped this sobering line: "The only difference between a rut and a grave is a tombstone!"

Put It in Perspective When everything goes dead wrong, as it surely will (that's a thing called *life*), put it in proper perspective. I remember hearing Rita Davenport say, "If money can fix it, it's not a problem."

Along those same lines are the words on a plaque hanging next to my phone: Unless it's fatal, it's no big deal.

Here's another of my favorites, by Masahide: Barn's burnt down . . . now I can see the moon.

I'm not, for one moment, saying you should, or could, make light of difficult problems or unfortunate events. I *am* saying that by seeing them for what they are, you can prevent the negatives from overwhelming or immobilizing you. You then have a better shot at digging your way out from under.

This old adage expresses it well: Humor is simply tragedy separated by time and space.

Or as my family has often said, "Someday we'll laugh at this."

Below is my favorite quotation regarding personal strength in difficult times.

> *"In the midst of winter, I finally learned there*
> *was in me an invincible summer."*
>
> —ALBERT CAMUS, AUTHOR

What's Your Purpose?

When I started writing this book, I soon realized it wasn't the snap I thought it would be. I fiddled and fussed till I felt I had nailed a key point. And what often sounded brilliant at night sometimes sounded like bologna in the morning. Some ideas didn't seem to fit anywhere. But I knew from the start that I wanted this message to be placed near the end of the book:

> *What you are doing is more important*
> *than what you think you are doing.*

Many of the bits and pieces of your business and personal life, the things you do daily, may seem mundane or of little long-term significance, but they're not. When you leave a light on for a late-arriving loved one, when you go out of your way to seek out the shy person in

a group, when you plan a birthday celebration for a child, when you give someone a sincere compliment with no personal agenda, you are doing much more that what you think you are doing.

The following experience brought this to light for me. As a comparatively new employee for a top direct sales company I had the exhilarating opportunity to work with a talented consultant to create a five-day leadership course for the sales leaders. This was heady stuff, a new direction that could either be a huge success or a huge flop. I was way over my head, but I was too naïve and headstrong to know it. After much head-butting, heavy discussion, tears, and laughter, we finally finished creating the course.

We were holding a "trial run" with a selected group of candid top leaders. The consultant and I were to share the role of facilitator. The first time it was my turn, I was consumed with fear and my partner knew it. He took me aside and asked me this question: "What is your purpose for today?" My mumbled answer was something like, "I want to do justice to the excellent material. I want the participants to feel like their time and money were well spent. I want them to go home feeling optimistic and inspired to make changes." I was holding a class, but what I was doing was more important than what I *thought* I was doing.

Was everything about that session perfect? No, but I calmed down and did a credible job. That one question took the focus off me and put it on what I wanted to accomplish.

Another personal example that occurred recently is when long-time friends invited us to dinner. It was almost a three-hour drive. And we would much rather have stayed home, puttered around the house, and relaxed after a busy week. However, we went, because sharing a few hours with people we cared about was more important.

No matter what you're about to do in your business, I'd bet that often you're carrying some sort of baggage. Maybe you're tired, you had a bad day, or things aren't going well in your personal life.

Maybe you feel ill prepared or apprehensive. When this happens, ask yourself: "What is my purpose for the next two hours?" What comes up for you will help you put your energy and your focus where it really matters.

It's calming and reassuring to ask yourself that question before business contacts, but equally helpful, and sometimes necessary, to ask it in your personal life. I have asked it at a very sad time, at the death of a loved one. I have asked it at a joyful time, an all-too-short visit with a dearly missed grown-up child.

But there's a bigger message. When you use the gifts you were given, when you live up to your potential, you go far beyond those daily things you do in both your personal and business life. You fulfill your purpose; and that purpose is to make a difference.

Making a living is necessary and often satisfying.
Eventually, making a difference becomes more important.
—DAVID CAMPBELL, AUTHOR